1997
PASSPORT TO
WEB RADIO

Music, sports, news and entertainment
from the hometowns of the world.

ISSN 1091-840X

 **International Broadcasting Services, Ltd.**

1997 PASSPORT® TO WEB RADIO

Our reader is the most important person in the world!

Editorial

Editor	Lawrence Magne
Contributing Editors	Tony Jones
	Rick Mayell
	Phil Schoen
	David Walcutt
Graphic Arts	Bad Cat Design
Sketch Art	Leigh Ann Smith
Printing	Quebecor

Administration

Publisher	Lawrence Magne
Associate Publisher	Jane Brinker
Advertising & Distribution	Mary Kroszner, MWK
Offices	IBS North America, Box 300, Penn's Park PA 18943, USA; World Wide Web: http://www.passport.com
	Advertising & Distribution: Phone +1 (215) 794-3410; Fax +1 (215) 794 3396; E-mail mwk@passport.com
	Editorial: Fax +1 (215) 598 3794
	Orders (24 hours): Phone +1 (215) 794-8252; Fax +1 (215) 794 3396; E-mail mwk@passport.com
Media Communications	Jock Elliott, Pickering Lane, Troy NY 12180, USA; Fax +1 (518) 271 6131; e-mail lightkeepe@aol.com

IBS Bureaus

IBS Latin America	Tony Jones, Casilla 1844, Asunción, Paraguay; Fax +595 (21) 390 675; E-mail schedules@passport.com
IBS Australia	Craig Tyson, Box 2145, Malaga WA 6062; Fax +61 (9) 342 9158; E-mail addresses@passport.com
IBS Japan	Toshimichi Ohtake, 5-31-6 Tamanawa, Kamakura 247; Fax +81 (467) 43 2167; E-mail ibsjapan@passport.com

Contents

Introduction to Web Radio

Communication's "Forth Wave" Takes Off

*I*n the beginning, our forebears communicated "long distance" to their comrades with shouts and hand signs, then extended the distance with drums and smoke signals. An individual might reach only a small number of people, but the process was interactive and democratic. After all, other folks could shout back and gesticulate with their hands, too. Just like on today's roadways.

Scribes and printing presses extended the reach and permanence of widely disseminated ideas and information, supplemented by roving troubadours bringing entertainment and teachings to distant villages. In this second wave, mass communication reached more people, farther, but at the expense of interactivity. Some told, most listened.

Then radio and TV were created, and for three-quarters of a century this third wave of mass communication has been one-way, wireless . . . and tightly regulated. Expensive, too, both for the equipment needed and to secure legal anointment to set up a station. Twentieth-century mass communication, like the period's workplaces and statist political movements, followed the *e unum pluribus* industrial model. A few told, but many listened, being satisfied with their 15 minutes of fame.

"Fourth Wave" of Communication

Until the mid-Nineties, the Internet really hadn't changed that. With its World Wide Web, the 'Net was a first-rate research tool and promotional vehicle, and with newsgroups became the ultimate electronic commons. But the introduction of streamed, or real-time, audio over the Web signaled the start of an entire new era whose profound impact is only now becoming apparent.

By 1995, streamed audio was being used by a small number of pioneering radio stations and others to extend the reach of their local signals. The results were pretty awful: quasi-intelligible audio, gaps of silence and frequent disconnects. But it worked, and by fall of 1996 much-improved streaming and the widespread installed base of 28.8 kb modems in place of 14.4 kb models resulted in

streamed audio of at least AM-radio quality.

What is taking place can scarcely be imagined. No longer is mass communication limited to one-way traffic in the hands of elites. As in the first wave of communications, Web receivers and transmitters are pretty much the same thing used by the same folks on the same level playing field.

How It Works

Already, there are hundreds of *bona fide* Web radio stations "on the air." Most use RealAudio, developed by Progressive Networks of Seattle. Of these, the majority still use RealAudio v2.0, which although intelligible makes for some pretty rough listening, even at 28.8 kb.

But the just-released RealAudio v3.0 has changed the rules of the game. Reliable, with audio quality that exceeds AM and sometimes approaches FM, it's available in both monaural and stereo—and it really works. Under conditions of Internet congestion, the worst that can be said is that it tends to echo or stutter, and occasionally pause.

That's because the Internet delivers its goods by "packets," which are like little packages sent through an electronic pipeline network using what amounts to "postal Zip codes" to tell them where to go. When they arrive at your PC, streamed and in the thousands, they are sorted into proper sequence so you can hear one uninterrupted signal, just like on an ordinary radio.

This approaches the ultimate in efficiency, which is one reason why the Internet is relatively cheap as compared to traditional delivery systems. But if the "pipeline" gets jammed up with too much traffic, the packets keep trying persistently to get through until an opening develops.

This creates two problems. First, the more jammed up the Internet gets, the more packets get stacked up trying to resend, which in turn jams up the 'Net even more. This "snowball factor" has led to doomsday forecasts of an Internet collapse, but so far Chicken Little's sky hasn't fallen. (If it ever does, look for a fast fix.)

Second, while those packets are waiting to get through, your PC isn't getting a signal. To get around this, "buffers" are used to store a little of the signal before it goes to your speakers. It's like a line of people getting into the front of a bus, filling it up, and after it's filled exiting out the back door while newcomers keep the bus full by getting in at the front. If some newcomers are late arriving at the bus, the back-door outflow can continue so long as the bus isn't completely emptied before new folks arrive. This way, the flow of people from the back of the bus is uninterrupted even if the flow into the front of the bus is inconsistent.

When the Internet is not crowded, your PC is actually storing a moment of signal—keeping the bus full. But when the 'Net is overcrowded and packets aren't coming in quite on time, the buffer releases enough of that stored signal for you to continue to hear it without interruption, so the "bus" gets progressively less full.

But if too many packets start coming in late, the buffer's storage gets used up, and you start getting a chopped-up signal. This comes across as "hiccups," echo or stuttering. In worst-case situations, you'll get complete silence while the buffer says to heck with it and reloads completely. Then, if the software isn't robust or enough "newcomers" don't show up, you may actually get disconnected.

This is what has made RealAudio's only real competition, Xing Technologies' StreamWorks, such a disappointing contender. StreamWorks, which is now in version 2.0, sounds at least as good as RealAudio under ideal conditions. But in the real world of congested Cyberbahns, StreamWorks hacks it only if you have a special wideband connection, such as ISDN, or listen when the Internet is relatively uncrowded, such as in the wee hours of the morning. Otherwise, it tends to have lots of annoying breaks in the sound, and sometimes even disconnects completely.

Looking ahead in a field this embryonic is foolish, but just around the corner is what may be the ultimate contender, VDOWave. Like StreamWorks, VDOWave is scalable and designed to handle not only audio, but also video, allowing for a single standard for both and for varying bandwidths. More to the point,

Using StreamWorks With Microsoft Internet Explorer 3.x

IMPORTANT: This sidebar contains information about editing the Windows 95 registry. Before you edit the registry, you should first make a backup copy of the registry files (system.dat and user.dat). Both are hidden files in the Windows folder.

At a Glance

The current version of Xing Technology's StreamWorks, version 2, when installed does not create the necessary entries in the Windows 95 registry to allow it to be successfully used with Microsoft Internet Explorer v3.x (IE3). In order to use StreamWorks with IE3, unless and until such time as StreamWorks is redesigned to function with IE3, it will be necessary to modify the contents of the Windows 95 registry to force the correct entry to be created when first accessing a StreamWorks audio feed.

Step-by-Step

To setup StreamWorks v2.0 to work with Internet Explorer 3.x:

1. Go to Web site http://www.xingtech.com/sw_now.html or http://streamworks.com/sw_now.html to download v2.0 of StreamWorks for Windows 3.1/Windows 95.

2. Once that download is completed, exit from IE3 and install the downloaded software.

To do this, double-click on "My Computer" on the Windows 95 desktop screen, double-click on "Control Panel," then double-click on "Add/Remove Programs." When the "Add/Remove Programs Properties" dialog box appears, click on the Install button within the Install/Uninstall tab. When the "Install Program From Floppy Disk or CD ROM" dialog box appears, click on Next. When the "Run Installation" dialog box appears, click on Browse, then locate the file SWPLYR2.EXE. Once you have used the file browser to find and select this file, click on Finish and follow the instructions on screen.

3. Click on the Start button on the Windows 95 task bar and select Run from the menu. In the command line field of the Run dialog box, enter C:\WINDOWS\REGEDIT.EXE and click on the OK button. This will load the Windows 95 Registry Editor.

From the Registry Editor menu, select Edit, then Find, to display the Find dialog box. In the "Find what" field, enter XDM, then click on Find next. This will locate the first of two registry key entries, My Computer\HKEY_CLASSES_ROOT\.xdm. Both of these entries need to be deleted. To do this properly, click on .xdm, then select Delete from the menu. *StreamWorks will not function correctly with IE3 unless both of these entries are deleted.*

Once these changes have been made to the registry, exit the Registry Editor by choosing Registry and Exit from the menu.

WARNING: Using Registry Editor incorrectly can cause serious problems that may require you to reinstall Windows 95. Microsoft does not guarantee that problems resulting from the incorrect use of Registry Editor can be solved. Use the Registry Editor at your own risk.

4. Bring up IE3 and connect to http://www.kpig.com/welcome.htm. From the top right hand corner of this screen, select the Live WebCast for the USA or Europe (elsewhere, try either). IE3 will download the file KPIG.XDM to your computer, then display a dialog box containing the following message:

> Internet Explorer is opening files of unknown type:
> http://www.kpig.com/kpig.xdm

In the section of the dialog box marked "What would you like to do with this file," select "Open it using a program on your computer," then click on OK. This will display the Open With dialog box.

In the "Choose the program you want to use" list box in the Open With dialog box, find and select SWPLAYER. If this entry doesn't appear in the list box, then click on Other. . . and use the file browser to select SWPLAYER.EXE. By default, it is installed in the directory C:\Program File\StreamWorks.

Once you have selected SWPLAYER in the Open With dialog box, make sure that the "Always use this program to open this file" is checked, then click on OK.

Support

Support, in a fashion, for Xing Technology's StreamWorks can be found at http://www.xingtech.com/technical_support/swplayer.html or http://www.streamworks.com/technical_support/swplayer.html.

Support for Microsoft Windows 95 and Internet Explorer can be found at http://www.microsoft.com/support/.

—Rick Mayell

VDOWave's parent company, VDOnet Corp., is now partially owned by Microsoft. Guess what *that* means!

Free Software

Some good news for those of us weary of paying for software upgrades: All the software you need for Web radio can be had for free, and very likely will remain free. Here's why. When Progressive Technologies indicated their RealAudio v3.0 would no longer be free, as v2.0 had been, there was a rush by users to find an alternative system. Within weeks, and hot on the heels of Microsoft's announcement that it had invested in VDOnet, Progressive Technologies backed off, claiming that they had never really intended to charge for v3.0, and that their announcement had been a "mistake."

Which is the best browser? The most serious contenders, of course, are Netscape Navigator and Microsoft Internet Explorer. Both are first-rate offerings, but Netscape costs $40 or so, whereas Explorer is free. However, for the purposes of Web radio, Navigator has the slightest of edges.

First, StreamWorks 2.0 doesn't function with Explorer, nor apparently does the relatively unimportant Internet Wave. Xing Technologies, which created StreamWorks, has posted a supposed fix, but only Houdini and StreamWorks designers are likely to figure it out. Even then, it doesn't really address the problem at the source, although the company promises eventually to come up with another fix. In the meantime, we've developed a proper and doable solution for this (see sidebar).

Second, Explorer can't handle animated GIFs and such. As a practical matter, this means you can't display World Time on your screen, but there's a solution for that, as well (see "What's the Time in Thailand" elsewhere in this book). However, one station in Keyser, West Virginia, has its live RealAudio page designed so that it is accessible only by Netscape browsers. Fortunately, it's the only station thus far which requires you to use Netscape if you want to hear their audio.

What's Coming Up?

Streamed video is only a couple of years behind in development. Like audio, it will benefit from the forthcoming 56 kb modems that are expected to be introduced later in 1997, and hold sway as the popular norm until early in the next decade.

Although cable TV systems have been hailed as the next great pathway to your PC, these probably will be used more to replace today's ISDN connections than 28.8 kb modems, and even then with wideband 1.5 Mb only for incoming signals (outgoing signals would continue to use 28.8 or 56 kb). But around five years from now, look for wide-bandwidth two-way connections by cable, fiber optic or something similar. That's when you'll find high-definition TV being made available from around the world . . .

and when you'll be able to set up your own "TV station" for the world to view.

Beyond that, where are Web radio and TV headed?

Right now, Web radio is a wired medium. But regular radio is wireless, so much radio listening is done on the move. Yet, what we think of today as "cellular telephones" is about to give way to a wireless lifestyle that uses a wide-bandwidth "wired" infrastructure to get signals from and to us, but as the last step will use a variety of wireless technologies to handle the initial and/or final hops.

MIT's Nicholas Negroponte, in what has come to be called the "Negroponte Flip," has predicted that by the year 2015 what were formerly wired technologies will be wireless, and what were wireless technologies would be wired. What now appears likely with the Internet is something of a double Negroponte Flip, where traditional microwave trunk relay towers are replaced by "wired" fiber optic, while the wired handset becomes wireless.

It'll be a "wireless wired" world, and the full power of the Internet—radio, TV and all—will be in your pocket or purse and car, meaning you can tune in Web radio while on the move. Those over-the-air radio and TV stations now used for broadcasting, along with satellites, could well evolve into wide-area packet distribution channels to seamlessly fill in reception and overloading "holes" in what will likely be, by then, a grid of millions of tiny cellular zones.

New technologies will emerge and

MIT's Nicholas Negroponte predicts that technologies that once were wired will become wireless, and *vice versa.*

help speed this along, but it's all feasible using existing technologies, expanded and refined. But here and now, today, you can catch broadcasting's fourth wave, and get the same thrill your grandparents did when they rode in their first "Tin Lizzie."

_____

Prepared by the staff of PASSPORT TO WEB RADIO.

"Information Era" A Hoax?

Perhaps, but Web Radio & TV May Be Winners

*L*ook into your conventional wisdom crystal ball, and you'll see the world's advanced nations marching out of the Industrial Era into a vibrant information economy. Ideas and facts will generate new prosperity, and goods will be manufactured by robots.

Perhaps, but before we rush headlong into this New Tomorrow, it might be worth asking where the money is going to come from.

Free for All

Take the Internet, currently the Mother of Information. Something very strange is going on, virtually without historic precedent: Companies by the thousands are vying with each other to give away information that formerly was sold. To lose money.

Not only that, they pay good money to set up and maintain Web sites so they can give away this stuff. They boast about "hits," but if only one hit in a thousand causes the cash register to ring, they call it a triumph.

Or they hope that things will turn around once they are set up for direct sales, or when they can find enough advertising revenue. But thus far many direct sales over the Internet have been a flop, and there are only so many advertising dollars to go around. Making matters worse, banner advertising at Web sites has been less than a sterling success—which shouldn't be surprising, given that Roper reported in 1996 that Americans were already starting to tire of being exposed to so much advertising.

Even if the Internet's "it's gotta be free" culture loses steam, there are so many players on the 'Net that increasing amounts of information are being provided simply for fun and fame. Information thus is becoming not the core of an economic revival, but a near-valueless commodity. Compare this to musty Second Wave days, when specialized experts with contacts, experience and smarts could generate new information and make money from their services.

Fast Facts

Related to this is that because the environment of change has speeded up, in part because of such developments as the Internet, information is valued more for its speed than its depth or excellence. The traditional concept of scholarship—the long delving into an area of expertise—comes up short against the fast and dirty answer, which is precisely what legions of interested lay folk can provide. For fun, for ego and for free.

Who'll Be Ahead?

But even in this strange marketplace, there will be winners. If somebody is thinking about buying a Jeep, what better way to be seduced than to click onto Chrysler's Web site? And there'll always be folks making money explaining and servicing these new technologies, as well as computer and Internet firms whose hardware, software and electronic pathways can turn a profit.

Web radio and Web TV should also have a sporting chance to flourish, just as have (sometimes) over-the-air and cable media. Although radio advertising and most TV advertising are based on local market ratings, and the Web is worldwide, rating tech-

Some Web applications don't make economic sense, but here's one that does.

niques and advertising focus can be adjusted. And instead of airing the same advertisements for all listeners and viewers, specialized ads in the same or different languages can be targeted to specific markets by using real-time information gathered through "magic cookies" and the like.

So, enjoy the World Wide Web. But also keep in mind Lyndon Johnson's admonition when being approached by city fellers with slick new proposals. "Shake hands," he used to say, "but put your other hand over your wallet."

—Lawrence Magne

Sports Scores Big on the Web

by Phil Schoen

Pittsburgh's KDKA had scarcely signed on as the nation's first radio station in 1920 when sports broadcasting got off and running. The reason sports succeeded then, and all-sports radio is a winner now, is simple: sports sells.

Now, all-sports stations are pushing beyond the boundaries of their broadcast area, trying to flush out new audiences in places Marconi could only dream of. Boundaries that today are without borders, thanks to Web radio.

With a click of a mouse, European supporters of Boca Juniors soccer club can hear every kick all the way from Argentina. Florida Panthers hockey fans can follow the puck, even when it's a continent away. And Duke fans in California can listen in to Blue Devil basketball as though they were sitting around the court in Durham, North Carolina.

The University of Tennessee's Neyland Stadium is home to the Vols football team. UT Sports Information

The Dallas Burn's Brandon Pollard outduels Major League Soccer's leading scorer, Roy Lassiter of the Tampa Bay Mutiny. Dallas teammates Zak Ibsen (far left) and Mark Santel look on.

Play-by-play might be the core of sports radio on the Web, but it's supplemented handsomely by sports talk. Dallas Cowboys fans can watch their team play on television, then hop to the computer in time to catch the post-game show on the radio.

While Web radio has a variety of formats with loyal and growing audiences, in many ways it is sports that is driving the wagon. Broadcasting to an audience that's only a phone line and modem away, the Internet has allowed fans from all over the world to follow their favorite teams. It's a trend that's mushrooming.

There are three major pioneers of sports "radio" on the Web: ESPN re-broadcasts much of what it airs on its regular radio network; AudioNet puts local stations' programming on the Web for distant fans to tap into; while SportsLine USA has created a sports radio network which, at this point, is broadcast exclusively over the Internet.

ESPN Expands with ESPNet

Unlike its competitors, ESPNet SportsZone already had a ready supply of ESPN programming to broadcast over the Web. "It made fuller use of our existing resources," says ESPNet General Manager Tom Hagopian, "and it was a way for us to increase our reach in the audio delivery business."

Hagopian says ESPNet simulcasts the core elements of ESPN Radio: the Fabulous Sports Babe every weekday, and the radio network's popular weekend programming. "However, we've had live audio on ESPNet that's not on ESPN Radio. We've broadcast college football, NBA games and college basketball," he adds. "We pick up the radio rights locally and use those on the 'Net."

For the most part, ESPN stays in the family, acquiring rights from its subsidiary, Creative Sports Marketing, which handles the logistics of radio network broadcasting for several major universities.

ESPNet has also worked out deals with local broadcasters for teams in the National Basketball Association. Hagopian says that when they first transmitted NBA games starting in 1995, "We'd do a 'Game of the Day,' but this year we have almost every game available. Some are limited to subscribers, but some are available to everyone."

SportsLine USA—
Web Radio Exclusive

According to Ross Levinson, SportsLine USA's vice president of programming, there are plans to distribute the service over "regular" radio stations in the near future, but the Internet will always be the core audience. "I think it will evolve. It's going to be something that grows," says Levinson. "If anybody believes that we're doing this for today, they're not thinking of the future. And with Web TV, cable modems and broadband trials, the audience will continue to grow."

It is an audience that's already grown beyond Levinson's expectations. Just four months after their August 1996 launch, listenership has increased more than fifteen-fold, about 200 percent ahead of where SportsLine USA projected it would be. And it continues to grow at a whopping rate!

At this point, SportsLine USA provides at least 500 hours of original programming every month, along with Penn State University football and the syndicated Sports Byline USA. Future plans include expanding play-by-play coverage of college football, and beginning coverage of college basketball.

Transmitting over the Internet allows for a wider range of shows that wouldn't be feasible on other broadcast media. For example, AudioNet carries a weekly talk show that focuses solely on the National Football League rivalry between the Green Bay Packers and the Chicago Bears.

SportsLine USA presents a talk show hosted by teenagers to get young fans' perspectives, and produces a popular "fantasy sports" feature. These are shows that would be difficult to get on a regular radio network. "That's what the whole thing is about," insists

ESPN

Drew Hayes is Executive Producer for the ESPN Radio Network, which is now heard as easily over Web radio as over the air.

sity basketball fans, but living in Dallas, Texas didn't afford them much opportunity to follow the Hoosiers' hoops exploits. That's when Cuban, a self-described "techno-geek," got the idea of putting radio broadcasts on the Web so fans could listen in almost anywhere.

Cuban says they weren't the only ones who were excited. "We did it just as a test to see if it would work, but response was just out of this world." Cuban is now the President of AudioNet, while Wagner serves as Chief Executive Officer.

Less than a year after it began, Cuban presides over a company employing 65 people, and the AudioNet Web site already records over two *million* hits a day. The company has moved out of Cuban's spare bedroom and into a converted warehouse in the trendy Deep Ellum section of Dallas.

As of 1996, AudioNet transmitted the games of 50 different college football teams, and more than 2,000 basketball games from over 100 different universities. College hockey and volleyball are also on the Web, along with Major League Soccer's Dallas Burn. Plans are in the works to get National Hockey League rights, similar to ESPNet's deal with the NBA.

In addition, AudioNet recently broadcast the German and Japanese feeds of the NFL's Super Bowl, and allowed fans to listen in to the press box and on the field. More than 30,000 listeners around the world tuned—or clicked—in. "For sports fans, we make the world a lot

Levinson. "We're trying to fill every niche out there."

And being on the Web can make it possible to fill several niches at once. "We can offer several different ways for people to listen," says Levinson. "As AudioNet does, we can offer a choice of eight or nine different programs to listen to at any one time."

AudioNet Founded for Sports

AudioNet began as somewhat of a lark in the second bedroom of Mark Cuban's house. Cuban and his friend, Todd Wagner, are big Indiana Univer-

smaller," says Cuban. "We tie you to your team. We tie you to your passions."

For now, AudioNet only transmits programming from stations and networks inside the United States, but that should change soon. "Absolutely," says Cuban. "Hopefully, in 1997 we'll have our first few international stations."

Why Sports?

What is it about sports that makes it so perfect for Web radio?

In a time when distant travel is commonplace, where even in many third world countries the prospect of moving to greener pastures becomes increasingly less challenging, sports remains a way of holding on to your roots. And it is Web radio that can keep those roots strong.

SportsLine USA's Levinson recalls a perfect example of this. During one particular talk show, the host noticed on his computer screen that someone had signed on in New Delhi, India. Requesting that he call in, it turned out the listener was a displaced Cleveland Indians baseball fan from Ohio, working in India, and using his computer to stay in touch with home.

"Sports is essential for the simple reason that sports has passion at-

Ted Eck of the Dallas Burn (dark shorts) struggles with Dan Calichman of the L.A. Galaxy in a 1996 MLS game at the Rose Bowl in Pasadena, California.

J.D. Cuban/Allsport

tached to it," says Levinson. "Anytime there's passion, there's an audience. And I think it will help drive traffic to the Internet as a whole."

"You can never get enough sports," contends Levinson. "Turn on the television every Saturday and Sunday and you'll have ten or fifteen channels with sports on it. We're just adding to the pie."

ESPN realized the impact of sports, and the potential profit involved, beginning their rise with the cable revolution back in 1979. ESPNet's Hagopian believes sports could be the key in the growth of Web radio in the late 1990s. "You need an element of urgency in Web radio, something you need to have right now."

While the introduction of RealAudio 3.0 has made Web radio sound like AM, Hagopian said, "I'm not going to go to listen to the symphony over the Internet. There needs to be a compelling reason to get on, because it's not the best delivery system."

SportsLine USA's Scott Kaplan—on air and online.

When it comes to sports, Hagopian contends listeners won't be so finicky. "If there's a game on that I care about, teams that I care about, then I want to know what's going on. In that perspective, sports works very well on Web radio because there's a need to know."

Where Is Web Sports Headed?

While he has faith in the future, Levinson says it will be at least 1998 before SportsLine USA's Web radio turns a profit. For now, it is a free added service to their full-service sports Web site. There has been interest from advertisers, but Levinson says advertising will have to wait until they build up the audience.

While Hagopian agrees the long term possibilities of Web radio are almost limitless, he argues the short term impact will be small. "It's an element that is complimentary. It's not something that drives people to the Web. It's the cart, not the horse."

"It's not a broad-based medium the way technology is right now," says Hagopian. "Innovations will help the growth, but in the short term, the next three to five years, this is no threat to traditional radio or television, because the audience is very small."

"The Internet, especially for audio, is not a mass medium yet. We're dressing it up and making it walk like it and talk like it, but it's not," admits Hagopian. "It will never be as efficient as radio sending out one signal across the country that anyone with a radio can receive."

Behind the scenes at SportsLine USA as it gets ready to go out over the Web.

However, Hagopian contends that doesn't mean Web radio can't serve a purpose. "This is less about huge events, as it is about more choice. It's not the fact that I can deliver that one game to lots of people, rather it's delivering a lot of games to a smaller audience."

Cuban believes the sky's the limit. "Think back twenty years and pretend it's 1976," he said late last year. "You wouldn't predict cellular phones, beepers, telephone answering machines, ESPN, CNN, Nintendo. And the list can go on and on."

"Now, you've got television, cable, and radio. After that, you've got noth-ing. We want to be that next broadcast medium," says Cuban. "The audience keeps on growing. Web TV could bring the Internet to the masses, and the nature of Web radio would change completely."

As it heads towards its 80th birthday, radio continues to include sports in a big way. It is likely that 80 years from now, sports will still be a major part of Web radio programming as well.

_____

Phil Schoen is an announcer at ESPN and WQAM-AM in Miami. Phil has written articles for a variety of sports publications.

Top Sports Sites

Hardly a day goes by when there's not at least one exciting game being aired over Web radio, plus behind-the-scenes action. Here are some of the best places to steer your browser.

United States of America

American Networks

AudioNet Sports. Dozens of college and university games are broadcast live over AudioNet Sports, along with professional teams. Between games, there are a variety of sports features from across North America. This site is a godsend for sports buffs. URL: http://www.audionet.com/sports/.

☞ Look for AudioNet's sports coverage to become increasingly international.

Drivetime *The Golf Radio Show*. On-demand news and interviews from this Monday-Friday brief network show for golf aficionados. URL: http://golf.capitolnet.com/.

ESPNet SportsZone. Live coverage of NFL football and NBA basketball games, plus on-demand audio from The Fabulous Sports Babe, SportsBeat, Radio Weekend, NFL on ESPN and a growing roster of other offerings. URL: http://www.espnet.sportszone.com/editors/liveaudio/index.html.

NFL Players Inc Radio. On-demand NFL commentary, prepared by football mavens at Fox and WTEM, Maryland. URL: http://www.sportsline.com/u/nflpa/nflradio.html.

Prime Sports Radio Network *Fox Sports Direct*. Sports talk and game

Clicking in KNBR on the Web gets you up-to-date information on a wide variety of professional and collegiate sports teams in the San Francisco Bay area.

coverage from around the country.
URL: http://libertysports.com/radio.htm
or http://www.audionet.com/radio/
sports/psr/.

SportsLine USA. Five hundred
hours a week and growing of live and
archived Web radio sports talk, plus
live college football and basketball.
URL: http://www.sportsline.com/u/
radio/live.index.html.

Winston Cup Today NASCAR.
On-demand interviews, news and
commentary about NASCAR racing.
Dozens of weekly half-hour and daily
five-minute shows are archived, going
back, like gestation, some nine
months. URL: http://
www.raceshop.com/wct/.

The powerful AM signal of San Diego's
XTRA, which actually transmits from Tijuana,
makes the Chargers, Bruins and Kings
audible throughout Southern California.

American Regional and Local Outlets

Web radio broadcast rights are evolv-
ing, so what stations broadcast which
games is subject to constant change.
However, as of now, here's the roster
of best bets for live sports coverage
and sports talk radio.

Arkansas

**KXRJ Arkansas Tech University,
Russellville.** Live college sports.
URL: http://broadcast.atu.edu/
media.htm.

California

KAVL Sports Radio 610, Lancaster.
URL: http://www.audionet.com/radio/
sports/kavl/ or http://207.113.204.163/
pub/kavl/kavl.htm.

KHJJ NewsTalk KHJ, Lancaster.
Possible live coverage of California
Angels baseball. URL: http://
www.audionet.com/radio/talk/khj/ or
http://www.khj1380am.com/.

**KNBR The Sports Leader, San
Francisco.** Coverage of the Raiders,
49ers and Giants. URL: http://
www.knbr.com/index.html or http://
www.audionet.com/radio/sports/knbr/.

**KSMC 89.5 St. Mary's College,
Moraga.** Live SMC sports. URL:
http://ksmc.silicon.com/ or http://
fermat.stmarys-ca.edu/~ksmc/.

KWNK Sports Radio 670, West Hills.
URL: http://www.sports670.com/, http://
207.113.204.163/pub/kwnk/kwnk.htm
or http://www.audionet.com/radio/
sports/kwnk/.

XTRA Sports 690, San Diego. Home
of the Kings, Chargers and Bruins, as
well as Jim Rome. URL: http://

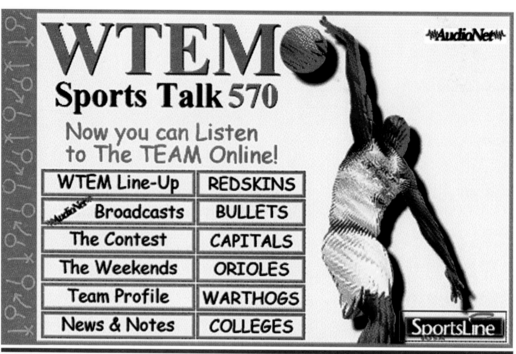

WTEM, just outside Washington, covers the Bullets, Capitals and Redskins direct and via AudioNet and SportsLine USA. Using the facilities of such major networks as AudioNet helps ensure there will be enough circuits for all fans to hear games on Web radio without getting a "server busy" message.

www.xtrasports.com/, http:// 207.113.204.163/pub/xtra/xtra.htm or http://www.audionet.com/radio/sports/ xtra.

Florida

WPSL *Talk of the Treasure Coast*, Port St. Lucie. Varying degrees of coverage of the Orlando Magic basketball team, Atlanta Braves spring training games, Jacksonville Jaguars football team, NASCAR and Indy races, Stanley Cup playoffs, the NBA, CBS Radio's Game of The Week, the NFL, and the World Series. Also, ESPN talk and interviews, as well as talk shows on golf and fishing. URL: http://

www.wpsl.com/, http:// www.audionet.com/radio/talk/wpsl/ or http://www.1stargate.com/services/ radio/starnetaudio.html.

WQAM *Sports Radio 560*, Miami-Ft. Lauderdale. URL: http:// www.wqam.com/, http:// www.audionet.com/radio/sports/wqam/, http://204.58.152.70/pub/WQAM/ WQAM.htm or http://www.1starnet.com/ services/radio/starnetaudio.html.

Illinois

WMVP *AM 1000*, Chicago. Live coverage of the Bulls, White Sox and Blackhawks at home and away. URL: http://www.audionet.com/radio/sports/

wmvp/, http://www.sportsline.com/u/radio/wmvp/teams.htm or http://www.1starnet.com/services/radio/starnetaudio.html.

Indiana

WIBC *The Voice of Indiana*, **Indianapolis.** Home of the Indianapolis Colts and Indiana Pacers, as well as Gasoline Alley's Indy 500 and Brickyard 400. URL: http://www.wibc.com/menu/html or http://www.audionet.com/radio/talk/wibc/. E-mail: (general) info@wibc.com or (Web project manager) bigjohn@wibc.com.
WUEV *University of Evansville,* **Evansville.** Live university sports. URL: http://www.evansville.edu/~wuevweb/.

Kansas

KJHK *University of Kansas,* **Lawrence.** Jayhawk sports. URL: http://www.audionet.com/radio/college/kjhk/ or http://www.ukans.edu/~kjhknet/tune-in.html.

Louisiana

KLSU *Louisiana State University,* **Baton Rouge.** Live Tiger sports. URL: http://www.cyberview.net/klsu/, http://www.audionet.com/radio/college/klsu/ or http://www.1starnet.com/services/radio/starnetaudio.html.

Maryland

WBAL *Radio 11,* **Baltimore.** Live Maryland Terrapins football and NFL Monday Night Football. URL: http://wbal.com/, http://www.wbal.com/ or

http://www.audionet.com/radio/talk/wbal/.
WTEM *Sports Talk 570,* **Bethesda-Rockville-Washington.** Live coverage of Bullets, Capitals, Orioles and Redskins games. URL: http://www.wtem.com/ or http://www.audionet.com/radio/sports/wtem/.

New York

WGR *News Radio 55,* **Buffalo.** Coverage of the Buffalo Sabres hockey and Buffalo Bisons baseball teams. URL: http://www.wgr55.buffalo.net/, http://ns1.moran.com/htmld/wgr55/,

There's no better sports coverage on Web radio than that given to North Carolina teams, including NC State football.

http://www.audionet.com/radio/sports/wgr/ or http://www.1starnet.com/services/radio/starnetaudio.html.

WOR *Radio 710*, New York. Rutgers University sports. URL: http://www.wor710.com/ or http://www.audionet.com/radio/talk/wor/.

WSYR *Voice of the Orange*, Syracuse. Live Syracuse University sports. URL: http://www.sybercuse.wsyr/ or http://www.audionet.com/radio/talk/wsyr/.

North Carolina

Carolina Panthers Radio Network, Charlotte. Live and taped Panthers football games, as well as other information, on-demand, about the progress of the team. URL: http://www.capitolnet.com/panthers/.

Duke Sports, Durham. Live and on-demand games of the Blue Devils football team, as well as a wide variety of on-demand feature programs about the team and other Duke athletic activities. URL: (news and features, all Duke sports, plus live football games) http://www.dukesports.com/; (live and taped football games) http://www.goduke.com/cyber/cyber.html.

North Carolina High School Football. Weekly live football game, available afterward taped, along with on-demand reports on scores throughout the state's eight high-school sports districts. URL: http://www.capitolnet.com/hs-football/.

North Carolina State University *Wolfpack Capitol Sports Network*, Raleigh. Wolfpack football games live and taped, along with reports on team activities. URL: http://www.capitolnet.com/ncsu/.

WRAL-FM *Mix 101.5*, Raleigh. Duke

SportsWeb 1000 News

Chicago's WMVP is no longer an all-sports station, but it still carries the Bulls, White Sox and Blackhawks.

University and University of North Carolina football and basketball, along with Winston Cup events. URL: http://www.wralfm.com/sound.html, http://www.audionet.com/radio/news/wral/ or http://www.1starnet.com/services/radio/starnetaudio.html.

WRAL-*TV* 5, Raleigh. Sports commentary, plus live games from North Carolina State, Duke University, the Carolina Panthers and the Durham Bulls. URL: http://www.wral-tv.com/sports/sportstalk.html.

WXYC *University of North Carolina,* Chapel Hill. Live and on-demand coverage of Tar Heel sports. URL: (WXYC) http://sunsite.unc.edu/wxyc/index.html; (Tar Heel Sports) http://www.goheels.com/ontheair.html.

Oklahoma

KTRT *Oklahoma Radio Network,* Tulsa. Live baseball. URL: http://www.ktrt.com/ or http://www.audionet.com/radio/talk/ktrt/.

Oregon

KFXX *The Fan,* Portland. URL: http://www.kfxx.com/ or http://www.audionet.com/radio/sports/kfxx/.

Pennsylvania

WTAE 1250 *Talk Radio,* Pittsburgh. Official station for the Pittsburgh Steelers, Pittsburgh Penguins and Pittsburgh Panthers. URL: http://audionet.com/radio/sports.wtae/ or http://www.wtaeradio.com/.

Penn State University, State College. Nittany Lions football live. URL: http://

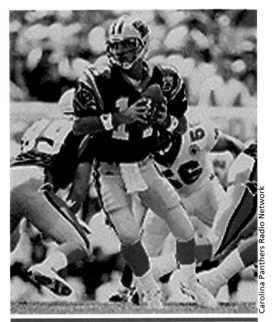

Carolina Panthers Radio Network

The NFL's Carolina Panthers can be heard over their own Web radio network, as well as WRAL-TV.

www.sportsline.com/u/radio/live/pennst.htm.

Tennessee

WHBQ *Sports 56,* Memphis. Live coverage of Memphis Riverkings CHL games. URL: http://www.audionet.com/radio/sports/whbq/ or http://www.flinn.com/56.html.

Texas

KAAM *620 AM,* Dallas. Home of Major League Soccer's Dallas Burn. URL: http://www.audionet.com/radio/classics/kaam/.

KTCK *The Ticket,* Dallas-Ft. Worth. URL: http://www.theticket.com/ or http://www.audionet.com/radio/sports/ktck/.

San Francisco's KNBR provides coverage of football's 49ers and baseball's Giants.

WTAW 1150 AM, College Station-Bryan. Play-by-play coverage of not only Aggies games, but also Longhorn contests. URL: (station, including Aggies sports) http://www.audionet.com/radio/sports/wtaw/ or http://www.wtaw.com/menu.htm; (Aggies sports only) http://www.audionet.com/schools/tamu/.

Utah

KFAN SportsTalk 1320, Salt Lake City. URL: http://www.audionet.com/radio/sports/kfan/.

Wisconsin

WRLO 105.3 Northern Wisconsin's Sports Connection, Antigo. On-demand daily comments from the Green Bay Packers' Head Coach. URL: http://unix.newnorth.net/wrlo/packers.htm.

Canada

Newfoundland

VOCM 590 AM, St. John's. Live St. John's Maple Leafs AHL hockey games.

URL: http://www.newcomm.net/sjleafs/live/default.htm.

Ontario

CFRA 580, Ottawa. Live coverage of the Montréal Expos, Ottawa Rough Riders, Ottawa Senators and Toronto Raptors. URL: http://www.cfra.com/ or http://www.3wb.com/listen.html.
CHIR-FM Greek Radio Station, Scarborough. Soccer from Greece, presented in Greek. URL: http://www.chir.com/noframe.htm.

Latin America

Argentina

Radio Mitre AM 80 LR6, Buenos Aires. Live soccer in Spanish, including the Boca Juniors Soccer Club. URL: http://www.clarin.com/index.html or http://www.clarin.com.ar/mitre.ram.

Brazil

Rádio Itatiaia 610/5970 kHz A Rádio de Minas, Belo Horizonte. Live soccer, presented in Portuguese.

URL: (click on RealAudio icon) http://www.itatiaia.com.br/som/index.html.

Colombia

Radioactiva Nacional 88.5 (Caracol), Santafé de Bogotá. Live soccer, presented in Spanish. URL: http://www.radioactiva.com/ or http://www.h-span.net/OTRARASP.htm.

Uruguay

Radio El Espectador, Montevideo. On-demand sports in Spanish. URL: http://www.zfm.com/espectador/.
Radio Oriental *CX12*, Montevideo. On-demand and live soccer games in Spanish, including Peñarol, Nacional and the Uruguayan national team. URL: http://netgate.comintur.com.uy/live.ram.

Europe

Greece

For soccer, see CHIR-FM, Canada.

Italy

Radio X *FM 96.8*, Cagliari, Sardinia. Live real-time update of the Italian Serie A soccer matches on Sunday afternoons, presented in Italian. URL: http://www.vol.it/UK/EN/SPETTACOLI/RADIOX/ or http://www.vol.it/RADIOX/2LIVEHITS/live.ram.

Portugal

Rádio Comercial, Lisbon. Live soccer in Portuguese. URL: http://www.radiocomercial.pt/audio/audio.html.

Spain

Catalunya Informació *Xarxa 4*, Barcelona. Soccer and sports results in the Catalan language, specifically the popular Barcelona and Espanyol clubs. URL: (live) http://www.catradio.es/cr/cr-direc.html; (on-demand) http://www.catradio.es/cr/cr-carta.html.
Radio Galega, Santiago de Compostela. Live soccer in the Galician language. URL: http://www.crtvg.es/.

Asia

Japan

JOER *RCC* Radio 1350, Hiroshima. Live Tokyo Carp baseball games in Japanese. URL: http://www.rcc-hiroshima.co.jp/.
JOLF 1242 AM *Nippon Broadcasting System*, Tokyo. J. League soccer in Japanese. URL: http://www.ipgn.com/JOLF/index-e.html.

PASSPORT's geographical chapters detail other stations with sports commentary and talk, such as KLIF in Dallas.

What's the Time in Thailand?

What happens if you want to know the time in the country you're listening to? After all, the station you're trying to hear in Kumquat, Malaysia, might not be responding because it's 3:00 AM over there. Or maybe you want to hear the Six O'clock Evening News, but need to know what 6:00 PM really is.

Midyear Madness

Sounds simple, but while you may change to Daylight or Summer Time, the time in the country you're trying to hear may not change. This can screw up the midyear time differential. And if the station is in the Southern Hemisphere, its time change may be the reverse of what happens in the Northern Hemisphere. A double whammy.

Trying to do it "my place against your place" can get so confusing that even the pros can get it wrong. One Asian station which is also on Web radio announces not only the local time, but also the time in Washington, D.C. However, some times of the year its announcements are off by an hour. To make matters worse, the time check is sponsored by one of the world's largest makers of clocks and watches!

World Time originated in England as Greenwich Mean Time. Even today, Big Ben's clock corresponds to World Time except during the summer. Digital Stock

Greenwich Mean Time (GMT)

Also known as Zulu Time

A very warm welcome to Greenwich, England - The home of World Time since 1884

GMT across the Internet:

FIND CURRENT UK TIME ALSO IRELAND, PORTUGAL	20:27:39 UTC CURRENT WORLD TIME	FIND TIME - MAJOR CITIES IN ALL TIME ZONES

- Greenwich Mean Time - US Navy version
- But heed the US Government warning!!

- **CURRENT UK TIME ALSO IRELAND, PORTUGAL**

- **FIND TIME IN ANY TIME ZONE ANYWHERE IN THE WORLD**

Why - even the US Space Shuttle uses **Greenwich Mean Time !!!**

Greenwich2000©

You can display World Time in many ways, including by going to the Greenwich 2000 Web site. All World Time sites work with Netscape, some with Internet Explorer 3.x.

Where You Are	To Adjust for World Time
Europe	
United Kingdom and Ireland London, Dublin	Same time as World Time winter, subtract 1 hour summer
Continental Western Europe; parts of Central and Eastern Continental Europe Berlin, Stockholm, Prague	Subtract 1 hour winter, 2 hours summer (for 1997, France may stay 1 hour summer)
Elsewhere in Continental Europe Belarus, Bulgaria, Cyprus, Estonia, Finland, Greece, Latvia, Lithuania, Moldova, Romania, Russia (Kaliningradskaya Oblast), Turkey and Ukraine	Subtract 2 hours winter, 3 hours summer

One Time for One World

The fix is easy: World Time, invented long ago in seafaring England so mariners could tell time no matter where they were. PASSPORT's station listings let you arrive at the local time in another country by adding or subtracting from World Time, also known as UTC, GMT or Zulu.

Now, all you have to do is set a clock to World Time. To do this, use the information below. Too "Second Wave" for your tastes? Go to http://tycho.usno.navy.mil/cgi-bin/timer.pl. This U.S. Navy site—those seafarers, again!—tells you not only World Time, but also local times throughout North America.

If you're using Netscape or another

Where You Are	To Adjust for World Time
North America	
Newfoundland St. John's NF, St. Anthony NF	Add 3 1/2 hours winter, 2 1/2 hours summer
Atlantic St. John NB, Battle Harbour NF	Add 4 hours winter, 3 hours summer
Eastern New York, Atlanta, Toronto	Add 5 hours winter, 4 hours summer
Central Chicago, Nashville, Winnipeg	Add 6 hours winter, 5 hours summer
Mountain Denver, Salt Lake City, Calgary	Add 7 hours winter, 6 hours summer
Pacific San Francisco, Vancouver	Add 8 hours winter, 7 hours summer
Alaska Anchorage, Fairbanks	Add 9 hours winter, 8 hours summer
Hawaii Honolulu, Hilo	Add 10 hours year round

browser that supports animated GIFs—Internet Explorer 3.0 doesn't—you can even have World Time show on your home page by going to http://tycho.usno.navy.mil/what.html. Another place for Netscape users to find out World Time is http://www.greenwich2000.com/time.htm.

Display Time on Screen or Separate Clock

The simplest way to show World Time would be to change your computer's clock and have it display on the screen. Alas, many operating systems don't allow for time in 24-hour format.

Where You Are	To Adjust for World Time
### Mideast & Southern Africa	
Egypt, Israel, Lebanon and Syria	Subtract 2 hours winter, 3 hours summer
South Africa, Zambia and Zimbabwe	Subtract 2 hours year round
### East Asia & Australasia	
China, including Hong Kong and Taiwan	Subtract 8 hours year round
Japan	Subtract 9 hours year round
Australia: Victoria, New South Wales, Tasmania	Subtract 11 hours local summer, 10 local winter (midyear)
Australia: South Australia	Subtract 10 hours local summer, 9 hours local winter (midyear)
Australia: Queensland	Subtract 10 hours year round
Australia: Northern Territory	Subtract 9 hours year round
Australia: Western Australia	Subtract 8 hours year round
New Zealand	Subtract 13 hours local summer, 12 hours local winter (midyear)

Cheap 24-hour desk clocks work well, though. Try the $9.95 MFJ-24-207B (800/647-1800 in North America) or the $14.95 walnut-framed NI8F LCD (800/431-3939, dx@universal-radio.com or http://www.universal-radio.com). Thumbs down on those fancy "World Time" clocks on jeweler's shelves, though. Extra money aside, the by-country time information they give is sometimes off by one or even two hours.

By the way, World Time doesn't change seasonally. To further eliminate confusion, World Time uses a 24-hour, rather than a 12-hour, clock, so 2:00 PM comes out as 14:00. Once you use World Time, you'll see why this 24-hour format is a godsend.

World Time = Web Time

World band radio stations, mariners and others who communicate globally have long used World Time, which has been around since the last century. The Internet has yet to settle on this, perhaps because so much PC activity to date has been within North America—a continental, rather than global, village.

But the time isn't far off when World Time will be displayed on virtually every computer screen. Unless, of

Bangkok's floating market is a major tourist attraction. You can hear Bangkok direct on Web radio's MCOT-FM.

course, Microsoft decides to make Pacific Time into World Time.

Prepared by the staff of PASSPORT TO WEB RADIO.

Compleat Idiot's Guide to Getting Started

*R*ight now, Web radio is where ordinary radio was back in the early 1930s, just as its Golden Era was about to emerge. It's new, exciting and just beginning to work great.

'Just beginning" means the autumn of 1996, when Web radio's original cacophony of distorted, wavery signals began to give way to reliable, good-sounding audio. Now, there are hundreds of Web radio stations of all kinds to be heard. Most are pre-existing AM, FM and similar radio stations that simulcast on the Web, but there are also Internet-only "stations" that are just like regular radio stations, but without radio transmitters.

Hundreds of radio stations now operate over the Web, bringing programs to the world that formerly were heard only by local or regional audiences.

TECHNOLOGY CORPORATION

The cutting edge of digital audio and video

StreamWorks 2.0 Now Available!

StreamWorks software is scalable, processing both audio and video. Under the right conditions, it can work well. But with ordinary modems and everyday Internet congestion, audio transmitted via StreamWorks often suffers from pauses and premature disconnects.

Programs Live or When You Want Them

Some Web radio stations are aired live, just like we're used to. Some others are only on-demand. On-demand stations store a handy library of pre-recorded shows that you can hear whenever you wish—like a video store, except it's audio instead of video, and you don't have to drive anywhere or pay for anything.

The best stations offer both live programming and on-demand archives, letting you choose whichever you prefer. In our listings, we identify which are live, which offer on-demand choices, and which provide both.

Listen While You Work . . . or Play

With Windows 95 and other operating systems that allow for multitasking, you can keep working at your computer the way you normally do, but at the same time listen to country music from Paris, Texas, or a discussion of mad cow disease from Paris, France. You can even browse the Internet while listening to radio on the Web, although your downloads may be slower or your audio pause briefly during heavy use.

Whether Web radio will cost you anything depends on the specifics of your setup. At worst, assuming you already have a suitable computer, it would run you around $500. If your computer is already online and appropriately configured, the cost could be as low as zero. See "What You'll Need," below, to find out exactly where you stand.

Fat Lady's Arm Bowls with Chickens

While most Web stations are from the United States, broadcasters in Europe, Asia, Australia, Africa and Latin America are joining in. Some are in native tongues, but most are in English. Hundreds are already operating.

The impact on programming is already beginning to be felt. On a 1996 talk show over a Salt Lake City AM station, the host spoke approvingly of the "Fat Lady's Arm" pub in New Zealand providing frozen chickens to clients for use as bowling balls.

Why? Because, he indicated, the station knows it has a significant Web radio audience in New Zealand from all the e-mail it gets, and the use of chickens as bowling balls has outraged some animal-rights activists in that country.

RealAudio, the Heart of Web Radio

Progressive Networks in Seattle has created RealAudio, a freebie software package that carries real time, or "streamed," audio through the Internet. Originally operating at no more than 14.4 kilobaud, like many new computer applications it tended to disappoint once the novelty wore thin. Even ordinary talk could be difficult to understand, and music was hopeless.

But now it's operating primarily at 28.8 kilobaud, the rate used by today's modems. Even more important, RealAudio came out with a new version, 3.0, in late 1996. The result has been a vast improvement, even at 14.4 kb. It's now to the point where you can hear stations in mono or stereo that sound as good as local AM stations, sometimes better. Most stations still use version 2.0, but this is changing so fast that by the time you read this, version 3.0 may have already become the norm.

AudioNet^{SM}

The Broadcast Network on the Internet^{SM}

Search the AudioNet Site

The AudioNet Programming Guide

Hot Software Deals

AudioNet, located in Dallas, is easily the most prominent Web radio network. Its roster of stations is mostly within the United States, with some in Canada, but they're also casting their eyes abroad. AudioNet's sports coverage is especially impressive, both for its scope and because its large bank of servers is capable of handling major listening peaks during popular games.

You can tell which is which right off. If a station sounds muddy and choppy, it's v2.0. If it sounds pretty darned good, but perhaps has some echo or "stuttering," they've gone over to v3.0. If a favorite station sounds poor, just send them an e-mail and ask when they expect to change over to RealAudio v3.0. Sometimes just a reminder is enough to get things moving positively. After all, station managers have lots on their mind, and can overlook something like this if nobody bothers to jog their memories.

RealAudio's other high cards are simplicity and reliability. Once you get to a station's Web site, all you do is click on the RealAudio or other obvious icon—when it's not obvious, our listings tell you what to do. In seconds, if the station's audio server is available and operating properly, the station is booming away and stays locked in. A handy volume control appears on your screen, too, and with Windows can be brought back up at any time just by clicking the RealAudio button on the taskbar at the bottom of the screen.

StreamWorks Used by Some Stations

A second major Web radio player is StreamWorks, created by Xing Technology of Arroyo Grande, California, which also supports Web TV of sorts. It operates audio from 14.4 to 112 kb, with the highest rate being for dual-channel ISDN connections. Its audio fidelity, baud-for-baud, is at least comparable to that of RealAudio v3.0.

But StreamWorks has many more dropouts—brief interruptions of silence—at 14.4 and 28.8 kb. It's also less user-friendly than RealAudio, and disconnects are much more common. StreamWorks is now in version 2.0, which doesn't perform noticeably better than the original version, but in other ways is worse. For starters, v2.0 lacks a volume control, which v1.0 had. And if your computer is set up for v2.0, it won't work on stations which have yet to switch from v1.0.

As if this weren't enough, StreamWorks 2.0 doesn't work with Microsoft Internet Explorer, one of the two most popular Web browsers in use today—even though v1.0 worked fine with IE3. Weeks after v2.0 was introduced, Xing Technology, the parent company, finally posted a fix of sorts on its Web site. But like much else that emanates from Xing, it is so poorly explained and convoluted to implement that even professional computer types get stumped. Xing promises eventually to come up with a better fix, but in order to get around this in the meantime, we've devised a step-by-step solution which not only addresses the problem properly, it's feasible for real, live human beings to implement. (See "Using StreamWorks With Microsoft Internet Explorer 3.x" within the "Introduction to Web Radio" article.)

The bottom line is that, for now, Web radio is RealAudio, and it's a smashing success. Its version 3.0 has allowed Web radio to cross the Rubicon from a pleasant curiosity to a mass communications medium of potentially historic proportions.

So that you can get off and running right away, here's what you'll need, and how to go about getting them without wasting money.

What You'll Need

• **Computer.** Your PC should have a 486 or better processor—any Pentium is ideal—and Windows 3.1.x, Windows 95 or IBM OS/2 for an operating system. For RealAudio, but not StreamWorks, Windows NT also works. Macintosh computers with PowerPC or 680x0 processors and an OS 7.x operating system are fully supported.

• **Audio Board.** Another "must" is a good audio board, along with suitable drivers/software—today's home computers often come with these already installed. If you use a PC, as opposed to a Macintosh, be sure the board is Sound Blaster compatible and 16-bit. Figure $90–300 for the board, plus an hour of tech time if you have somebody install it. Don't go overboard, but this is an item where your money is well spent.

• **Speakers.** Amplified and shielded computer speakers—$30–200—or headphones are a "must." Speakers last a very long time, and Web audio quality is improving dramatically. Either get cheap throwaway speakers

Download RealAudio 3.0

Listen to live and on-demand audio on the Internet over standard modems. RealAudio is broadcast-quality audio, including stereo at 28.8 & near-CD quality at ISDN.

RealAudio Player Plus
Order & download now

The full-featured RealAudio experience, including:

- Near-CD quality audio over modems with PerfectPlay.
- Scan, preset, and record.
- Option for a box & manual.
- 30-day money back guarantee.
- $29.99 for immediate download.

More information on RealAudio Player Plus

RealAudio Player
Download now

- Supports basic RealAudio functions, including stereo at 28.8 and near-CD quality over dual ISDN and larger bandwidths.
- Free for individual use.

RealAudio is the one popular audio streaming technology that really works, especially since version 3.0 was released in the fall of 1996. With ordinary modems, it is generally reliable, sounds at least as good as AM radio, and can even operate in stereo at 28.8 kb. It's free, too, although a $30 version is also offered.

for now, or do it right and go for something that your ears are pleased with when you hear CDs through them. A good investment.

• **Modem.** Your modem should operate at 28.8 or 33.6 kb. A 14.4 kb modem will allow you to receive some of Web radio's offerings, and if you already have 14.4, that's enough to get started—even if the result will probably disappoint. Many computers come bundled with internal 28.8 or 33.6 kb modems; otherwise, figure $100–300. Don't go for the gold here, as modem standards change quickly.

Just get something reasonable but not fancy, certainly nothing costlier than a USRobotics Sportster.

• **Internet Service Provider.** The first time someone hooks up to the Internet, they usually do so through a major online service, such as CompuServe or AOL, if only because these are so widely promoted. However, our tests show that those online services are unable to handle Web radio properly with some of their software packages.

For this and other reasons, experienced Web surfers usually hook up

Where do you want to go today? *welcome to*

Microsoft

News for You:

System Pro

Industry

Channel

Small Business

Web Builder

Developer

IT Executive

At Home

Games

Press

Shareholder

Education

Internet Service Provider

▶ **Comdex News:**

Windows NT Workstation and Windows NT Server Win PC Computing's 1996 Most Valuable Product (MVP) Award

- Microsoft Office also wins big: **The Best of the Best!**
- Here's hot news: Microsoft wins most creative booth at the Micrografx "Children Chili Cook Off at Fall Comdex". **Download our recipe!**
- Internet Explorer 3.0 wins 1996 **MVP Best Browser Award.**

▶ **Microsoft Announces the Release of Office 97**

Learn about the next version of Microsoft Office, the world's most popular office suite, and enter a contest to win prizes

▶ **The Best Implementation of Java for the Macintosh OS is Now Available.**

Download Internet Explorer 3.0 Beta 1 for the Macintosh with the Microsoft Internet Explorer/Metrowerks Java VM for Macintosh.

▶ **Win Free Travel in the Expedia 100 Flights, 100 Nights Sweepstakes**

Microsoft Expedia travel services makes it easy to plan and purchase the travel that best meets your budget and preferences.

▶ **Read More News**

solutions

Microsoft's Internet Explorer 3.0 Web browser is a vast improvement over earlier versions, and doesn't cost a dime. It works with Web radio, but doesn't support animated GIFs—a minor drawback. It does support StreamWorks 2.0, but only after some software gymnastics that should be cleared up in later releases of StreamWorks.

with local Internet Service Providers (ISPs), which are often better bets than major online services unless all you do is e-mail. To find ISPs, look in the most recent local phone book, or ask employees at nearby computer stores, Webmasters at local businesses or schools, or people who teach computer night courses in the community. *Your chief criterion should be how good they are at hand-holding—* avoid places that put you on hold, talk geekspeak, or give patronizing or formula answers. This is a highly competitive field, so you should be able to get a close-by ISP to give you *unlimited* monthly access for less than an ordinary cable-TV fee—$15–30 is typical—as well as top-notch service.

☞ Phone-line charges can be greater than your ISP fee. If you're going to be on the Internet for hours on end, having a flat-fee phone-line rate for unlimited calling between your place and the ISP may be cheaper than a per-minute arrangement. Call your local phone company for specific options.

☞ Although ISPs usually disconnect

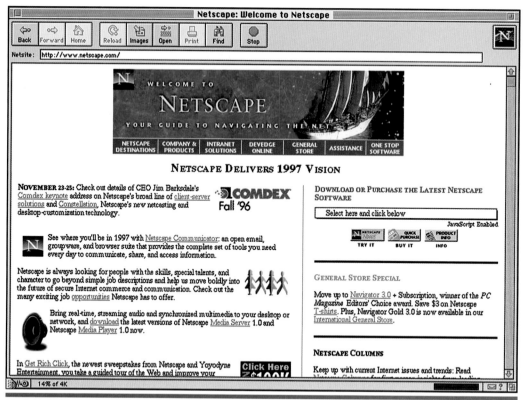

Netscape Navigator, the Big Daddy of Web browsers, supports Web radio without reservation. But it's not free, and chances are that its advantages over Microsoft Internet Explorer will diminish as Explorer and Web software applications begin to adapt to each other.

if you are inactive for 20 minutes or so, the incoming Web radio signal qualifies as "use." So as long as you're listening, the ISP connection to the Web will stay open. (Also, see the second 🖙 icon under "Web Browser," below.)

🖙 If you're using Windows 95 and CompuServe's Mosaic (e.g., with WinCIM), and want to change over to an ISP, be sure you choose an ISP which understands how to overcome Mosaic's overwriting of a Windows

DLL that needs to be brought back to its original state in order for the ISP to function reliably with your computer over time. This is a long and involved procedure which may require Windows 95 to be reloaded, but any ISP worth its salt will cheerfully agree to stay on the phone and walk you through the whole thing, step-by-step, while your hands tremble and your knees knock.

• **Web Browser.** The two giants in Web browser software are also

Sound Blaster is the technical standard for 16-bit PC audio boards, much as Hayes was once the standard for modems. Just as with modems, competing firms have begun to turn out compatible boards, often at attractive prices. Many new computers already come with Sound Blaster or comparable boards, and in the future this circuitry is expected to be integrated into microprocessor chips, making separate boards unnecessary.

among the best—Microsoft Internet Explorer v3.x (IE3), which is free at http://www.microsoft.com/ie/download/, and Netscape Navigator v3.x, which is $50 from computer stores or at http://merchant.netscape.com/netstore/NAVIGATORS/STANDARD/ITEMS/leaf/product1.html. IE3 and Netscape work with both PCs and Macintoshes. Which is faster depends on what's being done, but neither can overcome the Internet's slowness weekdays or a balky server at a Web site.

For Web radio, Netscape is the better choice if you are not technically inclined, as IE3 apparently won't work with the relatively unimportant Internet Wave, or with StreamWorks unless you make the modification we've detailed in another chapter. But if that doesn't bother you, then either browser will do just fine. Explorer, which is vastly improved in its present incarnation, comes in an earlier version bundled with Windows 95 and NT, but it's a snap to upgrade online to v3.x at Microsoft's site (see above). ☞ If you eventually have to reload Windows 95 for some reason, you'll also have to reload RealAudio 3.0 and Internet Explorer, as Windows 95 contains old versions of these that may overwrite the new versions you had loaded up earlier.

WELCOME TO MCAFEE.com
Network Security and Management
ALT.McAFEE

MENU

McAfee Mail
McAfee For Business
McAfee For Home
Online Support
Virus Info Library
McAfee University
Search McAfee
Download Software

**Secure your computer. Encrypt your data.
Click here**

Help keep the Internet Virus Free!
The Download McAfee Web Program allows visitors to your site to download the latest versions of McAfee products.

McAfee VirusScan outscores the competition in recent *Secure Computing* magazine Macro Virus Detection and Cleaning Shootout. Symantec Accused of False and Misleading Advertising; McAfee Demands Worldwide Recall of Norton Antivirus 2.0

Only the naive operate on the Web without good virus protection, and McAfee's WebScan is the best. Installation can be tricky, though, especially if you already have certain Norton software loaded on your computer.

☞ Your browser may automatically disconnect from the Web if you don't tickle the ivories every so often. This can be a nuisance if you're trying to listen without interruption, so set your browser so it won't disconnect. For example, with IE3 click on View, Options, Connection, then click off the arrow for "Disconnect if idle for . . . ," then click OK.

• **RealAudio Software.** The latest version, 3.x, can be downloaded for free from Web radio sites, or by going to http://www.realaudio.com/products/player/download.html. They also offer the $30 RealAudio Player Plus online or on CD-ROM (https://www4.realaudio.com/PP/index.html, or in North America phone 800/632-8920

daytime). But aside from some handy but forgettable features, it doesn't work any better than the free version. *RealAudio 3.x is an absolute "must"!*

• **StreamWorks Software.** This can also be downloaded free from its clients' Web radio sites, or by going to http://www.xingtech.com/sw_now.html or http://www.streamworks.com/sw_now.html.

☞ If you're using IE3, you'll need to follow up the StreamWorks download with the modification outlined in this book in "Introduction to Web Radio," unless StreamWorks indicates it has fixed the problem.

• **Web Anti-Virus Software.** McAfee WebScan is the best ($40, http://www.mcafee.com/), and it's worth getting their one-year online maintenance and support package for $49 so you can be protected against any new viruses that crop up. Downloading files from the Internet can introduce catastrophic viruses into your computer, so this is a "must." Even downloading zip/unzip shareware has been known to introduce viruses, so get WebScan first!

☞ Be sure to go over the Read Me file before installing WebScan, as otherwise you may have trouble connecting to your ISP.

☞ If you already have Norton Anti-Virus software loaded onto your machine, you'll need to remove all traces of it before installing any McAfee anti-virus product. Norton Utilities may or may not be compatible with McAfee, depending on your specific setup.

• **Optional Item #1:** Other streaming-audio software? You probably won't need them anytime soon. But if you come across an interesting site that uses something other than RealAudio or StreamWorks—these are identified in our listings—there will be instructions at the site on to how to download.

☞ Some may not download without problems, while others may not work with your browser. It's wise to back up your system before downloading any of these.

• **Optional Item #2:** Zip/unzip software to download audio material on file. This software can be downloaded automatically for free, when needed, from Web radio sites, if you don't already have it.

That's it, soup-to-nuts! Once you're up and running, turn the page and check out the hundreds of hometown and worldwide stations waiting to be enjoyed.

_____

Prepared by the staff of PASSPORT TO WEB RADIO.

Key to Icons Used in This Book

Throughout the rest of this book, you'll find detailed explanations of Web radio stations, broken down into five regions of the world. To keep things uncluttered, these icons are used:

RA288 RealAudio 28.8 kb, mono or stereo (as indicated).

RA144 RealAudio 14.4 kb, mono only.

StreamWorks StreamWorks, mono with everyday modems. Most stations shown as using v1.0 will be changing over to v2.0 shortly.

☒ Station also heard on World Band Radio. For a complete guide to the thousands of stations like this, see the current edition of PASSPORT TO WORLD BAND RADIO.

Passport to America

News and Entertainment from America's Hometowns

With most of the world's computer activity centered in the United States, it's hardly surprising there are more Web radio stations in that country than in all other parts of the world combined. Nearly every state has at least one station, and some communities already have several.

Virtually all types of music, sports and entertainment are offered, along with hundreds of local newscasts from the largest cities to small towns that are barely a speck on the map. Not surprisingly, most are in English, but a number of ethnic outlets are also making their presence heard world-wide, reversing the usual homeland-to-expatriate information and entertainment trail.

Because Windows 95, NT and a number of other operating systems allow for multitasking, you can listen while using your computer for other things— even while you're surfing the Web or answering e-mail!

Cattle graze at the Bruggeman ranch near New Almelo in northwestern Kansas.   L. Magne

Northern California's laidback KPIG is what Web radio is all about. It broadcasts rock, folk and other cuts you're unlikely to hear anywhere else, along with live Fat Fry concerts and "barnyard romance." Balky audio, though.

United States of America

World Time –4 Atlantic, including Puerto Rico and Virgin Islands; –5 (–4 midyear) Eastern, excluding Indiana; –5 Indiana, except northwest and southwest portions; –6 (–5 midyear) Central, including northwest and southwest Indiana; –7 (–6 midyear) Mountain, except Arizona; –7 Arizona; –8 (–7 midyear) Pacific; –9 (–8 midyear) Alaska, except Aleutian Islands; –10 (–9 midyear) Aleutian Islands; –10 Hawaii; –11 Samoa

LOCAL

Alabama

Birmingham

RA288 mono **WZZK Today's Hot New Country (when operating).** Country music from the heart of Dixie, where it all started. URL: http://www.bhm.tis.net/wzzk/audio/audio.htm. E-mail: wzzj@bhm.tis.net.

Arizona

Phoenix

(RA288) mono **KMJK *Magic 107.*** Urban contemporary/soul. URL: http:// www.audionet.com/radio/urban/kmjk. (RA288) mono **KMLE *Camel Country 108.*** Country. URL: http:// www.audionet.com/radio/country/ kmle/.

Arkansas

Little Rock

(RA288) mono **KMJX *Magic 105.*** Rock from the Sixties onward. URL: http:// www.magic105fm.com/index.html. E-mail: joelouis@ceinet.

Russellville

(RA44) **KXRJ *Arkansas Tech University* (when operating).** College sports, jazz, classical, alternative rock. URL and e-mail: http://broadcast.atu.edu/ media.htm.

California

Chico

(RA288) mono **KZAP *The Rock of Chico.*** Rock. URL: http://www.kzap.com/. E-mail: programming@kzap.com.

Delano

(RA44) **KDNO *Truth Radio.*** Christian conservative talk radio, including the disestablishmentarian ⊠ "Baker Report" and William Cooper's "Hour of the Time." Affiliate of the Amerinet network, which also includes world band radio station WGTG. URL: http:/ /www.audionet.com/radio/talk/kdno/.

Freedom-Santa Cruz

StreamWorks 2.0 (RA44) (RA288) mono **KPIG 107 *Oink Five*,** Freedom. Here's what Web radio is all about—first-rate programming that's original and rarely available over the air in places inhabited by normal people. KPIG, heir to San Francisco's legendary but now-defunct KFAT, is a one-of-a-kind station for aging hippies and kindred free spirits, featuring recorded and live progressive rock and folk music, interwoven with porcine pleasures and dollops of liberal news and commentary. Even the ads are sometimes a class act. Because KPIG live uses StreamWorks, which "hiccups" badly and tends to disconnect when the Internet is crowded, best times to listen are during the wee hours and weekends. Otherwise, take a break and go to their on-demand Comedy Archive, in RealAudio, streamed in quasi-audible clips at 14.4, or downloaded as one disk-hogging file with

WEBX

It's a wide, wide world. Listeners to post-modern WEBX 93.5 in Champaign-Urbana, Illinois, include Palma and Fabio from Italy, shown wearing matching station T-shirts.

worthy audio at 28.8 (or 14.4, if you prefer). For passionate porkers, KPIG offers its CyberSty ChatSpace for "gossip and barnyard romance." URL: http://www.kpig.com/welcome.htm. E-mail: sty@kpig.com.

Lancaster

RA44 KAVL Sports Radio 610. Sports. URL: http://www.audionet.com/radio/sports/kavl/ or http://207.113.204.163/pub/kavl/kavl.htm. E-mail: kavl@audionet.com.

RA44 KHJJ NewsTalk KHJ. News; talk; liberal disestablishmentarian Steve Marshall; and sports, including live coverage of California Angels baseball. URL: http://www.audionet.com/radio/talk/khj/ or http://www.khj1380am.com/. E-mail: cm@khij.com.

Los Angeles

RA44 KABC ABC RadioNet. On-demand audio of the latest Los Angeles area news summary, sports, weather and traffic from KABC via ABC RadioNet. URL: http://www.abcradionet.com/chicago.htm. E-mail: abcquest@abc.com or newsabc@aol.com.

RA44 KBLA Radio Korea. Korean ethnic. URL: http://radiokorea.com/homepage/radioko.htm, http://207.113.204.163/pub/kbla/kbla.htm or http://www.audionet.com/radio/international/kbla/. E-mail: info@radiokorea.com.

StreamWorks 1.0 KKLA Talk of Los Angeles. Christian inspirational. URL: http://www.kkla.com. E-mail: info@kkla.com.

RA44 KLVE 107.5 FM. Mexican-American ethnic programming, live and in Spanish, plus on-demand El Dicho del Día. URL: (live) http://www.h-span.net/livrasp.htm; (on-demand) http://www.h-span.net/GRABRASP.htm. E-mail: jesus@visatel.net.

RA44 KWNK Sports Radio 670, West Hills. Sports talk. URL: http://www.sports670.com/, http://

207.113.204.163/pub/kwnk/kwnk.htm
or http://www.audionet.com/radio/
sports/kwnk/. E-mail: feedback@
sports670.com.

RA288 mono **KZLA Southern California's Country.** Country music. URL: http://www.kzla.net/listen.htm or http://www.audionet.com/radio/country. E-mail: kzla@kzla.net. Toll-free phone (U.S. only): (800) 977-1939.

Moraga-Berkeley

RA288 mono **KSMC 89.5 St. Mary's College.** Rock, alternative rock and country music, along with live SMC sports, humor and information. URL: http://ksmc.silicon.com/ or http://fermat.stmarys-ca.edu/~ksmc/. E-mail: ksmc@stmarys-ca.edu.

Newport Beach

RA288 mono **KBCD Groove Radio 103.1.** Today's dance music and "the future of music for a new generation," live and on-demand. URL: (live) http://www.grooveradio.com/103.1/rebroadcast.html;

(on-demand feeds of syndicated shows) http://www.grooveradio.com/; (on-demand replays of archived shows) http://www.grooveradio.com/sound.html. E-mail: info@grooveradio.com, ena@grooveradio.com or eagle@grooveradio.com. Also see **KACD, Santa Monica**.

San Clemente

RA288 mono **KWVE K-WAVE 107.9, The Wave of Living Water.** Christian popular music and news from Pure Vision Ministries. URL: http://www.thegospel.com/radio/radio2.htm. E-mail: bruce@thegospel.com.

San Diego

RA288 stereo **KCR San Diego State University.** Alternative rock on this college cable radio station that hopes to add an AM transmitter soon. However, if and when it does go onto AM, the staff will start screening its music for obscenity and pro-

WVVX Rebel Radio features first-rate alternative rock, but even better is the on-demand Mosh Pit.

Uncle Ricky's TOP 40 RADIO REPOSITORY

Here's a dip into the past. "Reel Top 40 Radio Repository" consists entirely of deejay clips from American rock stations between 1959 and 1986.

fanity. URL: http://kahuna.sdsu.edu/kcr/. E-mail: (general) kcr@sdsu.edu; (feedback) kcr-staff@mail.sdsu.edu or http://kahuna.sdsu.edu/kcr/feedback.html; (Music Department) kcrmusic@mail.sdsu.edu; (Webmaster) webmaster@kcr.sdsu.edu.

RA288 mono **KFMB Star 100.7.** Eighties and Nineties rock. URL: http://www.histar.com/home_af.html. E-mail: knight@kfmb.com.

RA288 mono **XHRM The Flash (when operating)**, Tijuana. Rock. URL: http://www.theflash.com. E-mail: feedback@theflash.com.

RA44 **XTRA Sports 690**, Tijuana. Sports—home of the Kings, Chargers and Bruins, as well as Jim Rome. URL: http://www.xtrasports.com/, http://207.113.204.163/pub/xtra/xtra.htm or http://www.audionet.com/radio/sports/xtra. E-mail: feedback@xtrasports.com.

RA288 mono **XTRA XETRA 91X (when operating)**, Tijuana. Alternative rock and surfing updates. URL: http://www.91x.com/. E-mail: feedback@91x.com.

San Francisco

RA44 **CNN San Francisco.** On-demand archival clips, plus the Story of the Week—thin gruel, indeed, for the mighty CNN. URL: (archives) http://www.cnnsf.com/newsvault/index.html; (Story of the Week) http://www.cnnsf.com/storyofweek/storyofweek.html. E-mail: rockwell@turner.com.

RA288 mono **KCSN Jazz 91.** Jazz from public radio. URL: (if no response, e-mail station for latest URL) http://www.ituner.com/pilot1.htm. E-mail: (station) ray_smith@kcsm.pbs.org;

(Webmaster) kcsm@ituner.com or andrewb@ituner.com.

RA44 **KGO-TV ABC RadioNet.** On-demand TV audio of the latest local Bay Area news summary, sports, weather and traffic from Channel 7 via ABC RadioNet. URL: http://www.abcradionet.com/E-mail: abcquest@abc.com or newsabc@aol.com.

RA44 **KNBR** *The Sports Leader.* Sports talk, plus coverage of the Raiders, 49ers and Giants. URL: http://www.knbr.com/index.html or http://www.audionet.com/radio/sports/knbr/. E-mail: tweak@a.crl.com.

RA44 **KRON-TV** *News Center 4.* On-demand TV-audio news clips, mostly from the current day's reports. URL: http://www.kron.com/ or http://www.kron.com/frame_home.html. E-mail: (Webmaster) webmaster@kron.com.

RA288 mono **KTVU** *Channel 2.* Two three-and-a-half minute offerings of on-demand sports commentary, "Mark's Remarks," prepared by KTVU Sports Director, Mark Ibañez. Okay, we're cheating a bit to call this KTVU, since these Remarks may never have been aired over KTVU, but you get the point. URL: http://www.livesports.com/index.html. E-mail: (general) josh@servonet.com; (Sports Writer contest) http://www.livesports.com/sportswriter/contestentry.html.

KUSF *University of San Francisco.* You may love it or hate it, but this nominally Jesuit station's un-Jesuit programming is creative, interesting and one-of-a-kind. Mostly in English, it features "new music," varied ethnic music and news, along with community news and culture. URL: (KUSF) http://web.usfca.edu/kusf/indexbody.html, http://www.audionet.com/radio/college/kusf or http://www.1starnet.com/services/radio/starnetaudio.html; (BusStop Web radio community program) http://138.202.168.1/busstop/.

San Jose (also, see "Freedom")

Shockwave 28.8 **KOME** *Rock 98.5.* Rock and Howard Stern, but thus far airing only a few brief and uninteresting promo clips, rather than live audio, even though their home page indicates streamed audio "is up and

Los Angeles' KKLA features Christian programming from a Web site that keeps winning awards.

working." An Infinity Broadcasting station, but with all their resources you'd think Infinity would do better than this pitiful, cutsie showing. URL: http://www.kome.com/. E-mail: programming@kome.com. Toll-free phone (U.S. only): (requests) (800) 367-5663, (Loveline) (800) 568-3191 and (Howard Stern) (800) 247-8376.

Santa Ana

RA288 mono **KALI 106.3 FM** *Vietnam California Radio.* Vietnamese ethnic news, talk, interviews and music, live Monday through Friday Noon-4:00 PM PT, as well as on-demand. URL: http://kicon.com/VNCR/ or http://kicon.com/LUP/index.html. Fax: +1 (714) 534-9433.

Santa Cruz—see "Freedom"

Santa Monica

RA288 mono **KACD Groove Radio 103.1**, Santa Monica-Beverly Hills. Today's dance music and "the future of music for a new generation," live and on-demand. URL: (live) http://www.grooveradio.com/103.1/rebroadcast.html; (on-demand feeds of syndicated shows) http://www.grooveradio.com/; (on-demand replays of archived shows) http://www.grooveradio.com/sound.html. E-mail: info@grooveradio.com, ena@grooveradio.com or eagle@grooveradio.com. Also see **KBCD, Newport Beach.**
RA44 **KCRW 89.9 FM**, *Santa Monica College.* All sorts of features, including concerts, Hollywood Wrap and celebrity trials—but no live programming as yet. URL: (general) http://

www.kcrw.org/; (Hollywood Wrap) http://www.kcrw.org/hw/index.html. E-mail: webprod@kcrw.org.

TrueSpeech 28.8 **KRSI** *Radio Sedaye Iran.* Iranian ethnic news and talk in Persian. URL: http://www.krsi.com/.

Connecticut

Meriden-Hartford

RA28.8 mono **WKSS** *Kiss 95.7.* Rock and pop hits. URL: http://www.kiss957.com/. E-mail: savage@nai.net. Toll-free phone (U.S. only): (general) (800) 522-5477 and (requests) (800) 247-9570.

Norwalk

StreamWorks 2.0 **WEFX 95.9 FM** *The Fox.* Classic rock. URL: http:// www.internetwork.com/ radio2.htm. E-mail: http:// www.internetwork.com/ guestbk.htm.

Morning Show hosts Dave Smiley, Kim Morrison and Producer Matt do their weekday thing over San Diego's KFMB. KFMB

Stamford

StreamWorks 2.0 **WKHL** *KOOL 96.7.* Oldies. URL: http://www.internetwork.com/ radio3.htm. E-mail: http:// www.internetwork.com/guestbk.htm.

Delaware

Wilmington

RA44 **WDEL 1150.** Talk, news. URL: http://www.wdel.com/ or http:// www.audionet.com/radio/talk/wdel/. E-mail: wdel@ravenet.com.

District of Columbia

RA44 **C-SPAN.** If you're an American without cable TV, or living outside the United States, C-SPAN will bring you on Web radio, live and uncut, into all sorts of official Government proceedings in Washington. On-demand features and speeches, too, including the Weekly Radio Journal. URL: (live, when on) http://www.c-span.org/event.htm; (on-demand) http://www.c-span.org/ realaudi.html. E-mail: viewer@c-span.org.

StreamWorks 2.0 **France Fréquence.** See **France**.

WMET and WTEM—see **Maryland**.

WUST 1120 AM—see **New World Chronicle** under National/International. Nothing else offered over Web radio.

Florida

Jacksonville

StreamWorks 2.0 **Continental Cablevision Jacksonville Jaguars.** Live broadcasts of Jacksonville Jaguars football games, nothing more for now. URL: http:// www.jaguars.com/jag_web/yourcall/ broadcast_off.htm. E-mail: (team) http://www.jaguars.com/jag_web/ yourcall/broadcast_off.htm; (Webmaster) raminfo@ramworks.com.

Melbourne Beach-Inglis

RA28.8 mono **WAVQ** *Relax 104.3.* Easy listening, which has proven to be a surprisingly popular format over the

Web. URL: http://www.relaxradio.com/.
E-mail: relax@relaxradio.com.

Miami-Miami Beach-Hollywood-Ft. Lauderdale

(RA44) Miami Christian University, Miami. Live and on-demand Christian music, religious services and talks from this Internet-only college station affiliated with the CIRnet network. URL: http://www.mcu.edu/radio/. E-mail: revrick@jf.org.

(RA288) mono **WLVE 93.9 FM** *Love 94*, Miami Beach-Ft. Lauderdale. Smooth jazz, presented live. URL: http://www.audionet.com/radio/jazz/wlve/. E-mail (specify WLVE in subject line): http://www.949zeta.com/ZMAILA.HTM.

(RA44) WZTA 94.9 ZETA, Miami Beach-Ft. Lauderdale. Formula alternative rock. URL: http://www.949zeta.com/text.htm. E-mail: http://www.949zeta.com/ZMAILA.HTM.

(RA44) WQAM *Sports Radio 560*, Hollywood. Sports, including live coverage of the Florida Panthers Hockey team. WQAM's broadcasts of the Florida Marlins baseball team, Fabulous Sports Babe and Rush Limbaugh Show are not carried via the Web, leaving only dead air during these blocked-out periods. If you call (1-954/435-0560) and tell them you are listening on AudioNet, you'll be the next caller to go on the air. URL: http://www.wqam.com/, http://www.audionet.com/radio/sports/wqam/, http://204.58.152.70/pub/WQAM/WQAM.htm or http://www.1starnet.com/services/radio/starnetaudio.html. E-mail: wqam@audionet.com or http://www.wqam.com/.

Port St. Lucie

(RA44) WPSL *Talk of the Treasure Coast.* Here's a station that's got it right, even if its Web visuals are uninspiring. Live talk, news and sports, *plus* on-demand shows. Varying degrees of coverage of the Orlando Magic basketball team, Atlanta Braves spring training games, Jacksonville Jaguars football team, NASCAR and Indy races, Stanley Cup playoffs, the NBA, CBS Radio's Game of The Week, the NFL, and the World Series. Also, ESPN talk and interviews, as well as talk shows on golf and fishing. This has to be a favorite among snowbirds during the summer, and makes for first-rate listening for others year-round. URL: http://

Listen to Relax 104.3 The World's First Easy Listening Radio Station That You Can Listen To Anywhere in the World!

Florida's WAVQ is one of the relatively few stations to bring easy listening music to the Web. Surprisingly popular, too.

www.wpsl.com/, http://
www.audionet.com/radio/talk/wpsl/
or http://www.1stargate.com/services/
radio/starnetaudio.html. E-mail:
wpsl@gate.net.

Tampa Bay

WFLA *Newsradio 970*. This station is playing a D-minus version of
"I've Got A Secret." News, talk and a
wide variety of otherwise rarely heard
sports material, *but* the only audio
consists of montage promo clips—
nary a peep live, notwithstanding the
legions of snowbirds and others who'd
listen from afar if they had the chance.
URL: http://www.970wfla.com/
home.html. E-mail: newsradio@
wfla.com. Toll-free phone (U.S. only):
(800) 969-9352.

WMTX *Mix 96*. Adult
contemporary top-40 hits. URL: http://
www.audionet.com/radio/
contemporary/wmtx.

Georgia

Atlanta

WKLS *96 Rock*. Southern-
oriented rock, which makes this station
stand nicely out from the herd of for-
mula-rock offerings. URL: http://
www.96rock.com/ or http://
www.audionet.com/radio/rock/wkls/.
E-mail: amys@96rock.com.

WNNX *99X*. Alternative rock.
URL: http://www.com/99x/index/html
or http://www.audionet.com/radio/
alternative/wnnx.

Augusta

mono WCHZ *Z95*. Alternative rock.
URL: http://www.csra.net/z95 or http://
www.audionet.com/radio/alternative/
wchz/. E-mail: melissa@csra.net.

Hawaii

Kihei, Maui

**stereo KONI 104.7 FM *The Heart-
beat*.** Today's top pop, soul and other
light hits, live and on-demand. Even
better, for those seeking some great
Hawaiian music—not tourist stuff, but
original and creative Hawaiian offerings—is the separate Web site "Hawaiian Jamz," operated by KONI's
operations manager. URL: (station)
http://www.mauigateway.com/koni/
htm; (Hawaiian Jamz) http://
www.mauigateway.com/hwnintro.htm.
E-mail: koni@mauigateway.com.

Top Cops Gary Wilson and Theresa Woodson
of the Port St. Lucie Police Department air
"Cop Talk" every Tuesday at 6:20 PM ET
(World Time 2220 summer, 2320 winter)
over WPSL.

Illinois

Champaign-Urbana

RA288 stereo **WEBX *The Web 93.5.*** Here's one post-modern rock station that's doing unusually well on the Web, plus its site has lots of helpful links to community and University of Illinois activities, restaurants and the like. URL: http://www.webxfm.com/webaudio.html. E-mail: bsaldeen@webxfm.com.

Chicago

RA144 **WLS AM-890 *ABC RadioNet.*** On-demand audio of the latest local Chicago news summary, sports, weather and traffic from WLS via ABC RadioNet. Also, each Saturday there's the popular Tech Talk, hosted by Ken Rutkowski. URL: (all, including Tech Talk live) http://www.abcradionet.com/chicago.htm; (Tech Talk, on-demand) http://www.ttalk.com/html/main.html. E-mail: (general) abcquest@abc.com or newsabc@aol.com; (Tech Talk) ken@ttalk.com.

Share your weekend nights with Malone on San Diego's Star 100.7 as she teases punsters with, "I'm Malone." KFMB

RA288 mono **WMVP *Sports Radio 1000.*** Sports, including—oh, *yaas!*—live coverage of the Bulls, White Sox and Blackhawks at home and away. URL: http://www.audionet.com/radio/sports/wmvp/, http://www.sportsline.com/u/radio/wmvp/teams.htm or http://www.1starnet.com/services/radio/starnetaudio.html. E-mail: wmvp@audionet.com. Toll-free phone (U.S. only) (800) 746-9472.

RA288 mono **WNVR-1030 *Polnet*,** Vernon Hills. A variety of ethnic programs, live and on-demand: **Polskie Radio Chicago**, **Russian Radio Chicago**, **Austrian & German Radio Chicago** [including programming from the % **Österreicher Rundfunk (ORF)** in Austria], the **Arab Network of America**, **Bulgarian Radio Chicago** and **Serbian Radio**. Sister station to WKTA, Evanston. URL: http://www.pclradio.com/.E-mail: pcl@radioz.com.

RA144 **WVVX/WKTA *Rebel Radio*,** Highland Park-Evanston-Northbrook. Here's where you'll find Rebel Radio, one of the best alternative rock experiences around, with both live and on-demand offerings. Be sure to click on the Mosh Pit button, while checking out Mr. Dead on the screen. URL: http://www.rebelradio.com/. E-mail: rebel@rebelradio.com.

Peoria

RA288 stereo **RA288** mono **RA144** **WWCT-FM 105.7 *Rock 106.*** Today's rock, live plus on-demand CDs. Nominally phasing out 14.4 in favor of 28.8 stereo, but as of press time was in 28.8 mono. URL:

The Talk of The Treasure Coast
Port St. Lucie, FL

Here's SportsTalk that's so pleasant, you wonder why more stations don't emulate it. The only catch is that its considerable lineup of sports coverage on AM could be kept off Web radio by rights requirements.

(click at bottom of page) http://www.rock106.com/listen.htm. E-mail: hirsch@rock106.com.

Indiana

Evansville

StreamWorks 2.0 **WUEV University of Evansville.** Jazz and blues, live university sports and international broadcasts via World Radio Network. Live and on-demand news, although the on-demand offering sometimes airs music, instead. URL: http://www.evansville.edu/~wuevweb/. E-mail: http://www.evansville.edu/~wuevweb/make-request.html.

Indianapolis

RA288 WIBC The Voice of Indiana. News, sports and talk. Home of the Indianapolis Colts and Indiana Pacers, as well as Gasoline Alley's Indy 500 and Brickyard 400. URL: http://www.wibc.com/menu/html or http://www.audionet.com/radio/talk/wibc/.

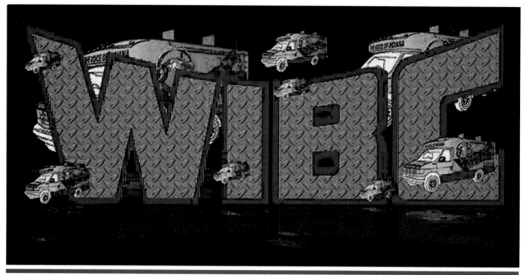

"The Voice of Indiana" hails from Indianapolis, with statewide news, sports and talk. Indy races, too, so long as they hold Web radio rights.

E-mail: (general) info@wibc.com or (Web project manager) bigjohn@wibc.com.

(RA288) WTLC-AM, WTLC-FM and WGLD *Solid Gold Soul.* These urban contemporary stations are on the Web from the same site. That makes this the ultimate link for music that is badly under-represented or absent in most radio markets. URL: http://www.wtlc.com or http://www.audionet.com/radio/urban/wtlc/. E-mail: (general) wtlc@stlc.com, (vice president) pmajor@iquest.net.

Scottsburg

(RA288) mono WMPI *I105.3.* What a pleasure to find a country music station that's actually in a small town "out thar" in the countryside! Rural southeastern Indiana's WMPI offers contemporary and classic cuts live, along with enough local news and weather to gladden the hearts of homesick small-town Hoosier exiles everywhere. URL: http://www.scottsburg.com/i1053/i105.htm. E-mail: wmpi@scottsburg.com.

Iowa

Statewide

(RA44) Radio Iowa *Iowa's News Source.* On-demand Iowa news, as well as high school and other Iowa sports reports from this statewide radio network. URL: (news) http://www.radioiowa.com/news.html; (sports) http://www.radioiowa.com/sports.htm. E-mail: info@radioiowa.com.

Local

Cedar Rapids

RA44 KCRG *News Radio 1600 AM/* **KCRG** *TV 9.* On-demand news headlines and weather for Eastern Iowa, but no live offering. URL: (news) http://www.kcrg.com/news/knews.htm; (weather) http://www.kcrg.com/weather/kweath.htm. E-mail: (general) newsroom@kcrg.com; (Webmaster) 90online@kcrg.com.

Kansas

Kansas City

RA44 KCTV *Channel 5*—see **Missouri.**

Lawrence

RA288 mono **KJHK** *University of Kansas.* KU Jayhawk sports, live and recorded music, and Kansas news. A "must hear" station for Jayhawk sports fans, Kansas expats and diaspora KU alumni. URL: http://www.audionet.com/radio/college/kjhk/ or http://www.ukans.edu/~kjhknet/tune-in.html. E-mail: (music requests) http://www.ukans.edu/~kjhknet/email/request_form.html; (Webmaster) http://www.ukans.edu/~kjhknet/email/technical_form.html.

Wichita

RA288 mono **KTLI** *Light 99 FM.* Contemporary light Christian music, with no local news except at the half hour weekdays from 6:00 through 9:00 AM CT. Some Christian stations sound as if they are talking to children, but not so this station, which except for the lyrics sounds like a typical commercial "lite" station. URL: http://www.southwind.net/ktli/live.html. E-mail: (general) light99@southwind.net; (Webmaster) bob@southwind.net.

Kentucky

Lexington

RA44 WVLK *Stereo AM Radio 59.* This station is fulltime news and sports, which would be great to hear worldwide. Alas, currently over the Web the only offering is University of Kentucky Wildcat sports, transmitted live. URL: http://www.audionet.com/schools/uky/, http://www.uksports.com/listen/ or http://www.mis.net/wvlkam/. E-mail: ukinfo@uksports.com or ukvin@uksports.com.

Louisiana

Baton Rouge

RA44 KLSU *Louisiana State University.* Alternative rock, live LSU Tiger sports. URL: http://www.cyberview.net/klsu/, http://www.audionet.com/radio/college/klsu/ or http://www.1starnet.com/services/radio/starnetaudio.html. E-mail: klsu91@cyberview.net.

Hammond

RA288 mono **KSLU** *90.9 FM Southeastern Louisiana University.* A wide variety of public radio programs, plus jazz, blues, Louisiana music and classical concerts. E-mail: ipitzer@I-55.com.

New Orleans

(RA288) mono **WWOZ *The Sound of New Orleans***, Metairie. A delightful gumbo of live and on-demand jazz, Delta and other blues, R&B, cajun, zydeco, gospel, Caribbean, Brazilian and Latin music makes this volunteer-operated station one of Web radio's gems. With luck, perhaps someday they will go to RealAudio 28.8 stereo so that the sound quality can be worthy of their incredible music. URL: http://www.wwoz.org or http://www.audionet.com/radio/jazz/wwoz/. E-mail: wwoz@gnofn.org.

Maryland

Baltimore

(RA288) mono **WBAL Radio 11.** Award-winning news, talk and sports talk, as well as live Maryland Terrapins football and NFL Monday Night Football. URL: http://wbal.com/, http://www.wbal.com/ or http://www.audionet.com/radio/talk/wbal/. E-mail: news@wbal.com. Toll-free phone (U.S. only): (800) 767-9225.

Bethesda-Rockville-Washington

(RA44) **WTEM *Sports Talk 570.*** Sports chat, plus live coverage of Bullets,

Capitals, Orioles and Redskins games. Home weekdays to "Imus In The Morning." URL: http://www.wtem.com/ or http://www.audionet.com/radio/sports/wtem/. E-mail: tcastle@erols.com.

Gaithersburg-Washington

(RA44) **WMET *1150 AM.*** News, business news and talk. URL: http://www.audionet.com/radio/talk/wmet/. E-mail: wmet@audionet.com.

Massachusetts

Boston

(RA44) **WGBH-FM 89.7.** "No Soap Radio," a half-hour on-demand comedy. Currently, nothing else is being offered over Web radio from the estimable WGBH organization. URL: http://198.147.175.20/wgbh/pages/radio/nosoap/. E-mail: feedback@wgbh.org or http://www.boston.com/wgbh/forms/feedbackform.html.

KLSU airs Louisiana State University sports and alternative rock—all live.

Michigan

Kalamazoo

(RA44) **WKZO *Newstalk Radio.*** On-demand audio of the last-aired news, including business and financial news, plus sports, weather and farm report via the Kalamazoo County Chamber of Commerce. No live audio. URL: http://www.kazoobiz.com/enterp/

kzo.htm. E-mail:
enterprise@sapien.net.
RA288 **WRKR** *The Rocker.* Rock, but
sound clips *only.* URL: http://
www.wrkr.com/. E-mail:
winter@wrkr.com.

Minnesota

Minneapolis

StreamWorks 2.0 **KEGE 93.7 EDGE.**
Alternative rock. URL: http://
www.937edge.com/live/index.html.
E-mail: edge@usinternet.com.

St. Paul

RA44 Shockwave 28.8 **Minnesota Public
Radio.** Yes, wannabe Norwegian
bachelors and others can hear—and
see bits of—"A Prairie Home Companion" live on the Web, although the site
tends to get jammed up Saturday
evenings from 6 – 8 PM ET, when the
show is on. Fortunately, you can also
get an audio rundown of the prior
show's performance on-demand,
when bandwidth is more available.
Remember, there's other on-demand
material from MPR besides Garrison
Keillor's weekly offering, so them a
try, too. URL: (MPR, all programs)
http://www.mnonline.org/mpr/; (Prairie Home Companion, live Saturday
evenings) http://www.mnonline.org/
mpr/cgi-bin/index.cgi; (Prairie Home
Companion, prior show on-demand)
http://www.mnonline.org/wobegon/
index.html. E-mail: (MPR)
mail@mpr.org; (Prairie Home Companion) phc@mpr.org. Toll-free phone

Host Stacey West brings Texas pizzaz to
KPLX's country music lineup.

(working hours, U.S. only): (MPR)
(800) 228-7123; (Prairie Home Companion shop) (800) 998-8173.

Mississippi

Clinton-Jackson

RA44 **WHJT** *Alive 93.5,* **Mississippi
College.** If you've found non-gospel
Christian music to be boring, try this
nonprofit station's relatively energized
style of inspirational music. Audio is
live, of course, but an interesting twist

WHJT

Robin Tanksley manages Mississippi's only Web radio station, WHJT in Clinton-Jackson. It's also got the liveliest Christian music on the Web.

is that they also offer the previous day's programming "live on tape" with a 24-hour delay. Some earlier on-demand clips, too, along with an award-winning Web site. Affiliated with the CIRnet network. URL: http://www.mc.edu/~alive935/live.html. E-mail: tanksley@mc.edu.

Missouri

Kansas City

RA44 **KCTV Channel 5.** TV audio, for now only of the 10 PM newscast. URL: http://www.kctv.com/whatsnew.htm or http://www.kctv.com/. E-mail: (general) kctu@kctv.com, (Webmaster) ander@kctv.com.

St. Louis

RA288 mono **KXOK *The Soul of St. Louis.*** St. Urban contemporary/soul. URL: http://www.kxok.com/ or http://www.audionet.com/radio/urban/. E-mail: kxok@audionet.com.

Nevada

Las Vegas

RA44 **KDWN *K-DAWN* 720 AM.** Talk, but with Rush Limbaugh omitted from the station's Web offering. URL: http://www.audionet.com/radio/talk/kdwn/. **RA288** mono **KOOL *Vegas Radio.*** Rock, along with live and on-demand medical and chiropractic tips. URL: http://www.vegasradio.com/kool.html.

New Jersey

Statewide

RA288 mono **WKXW/WBBS *New Jersey 101.5* (when reactivated)**, Trenton-Millville-Atlantic City. New Jersey news, traffic and weather, plus personal talk and classic rock. URL: http://www.nj1015.com/ or http://www.nj1015.com/index.html. E-mail: nj1015@nj1015.com.

Local

Dumont-Fort Lee

RA288 mono **WJUX *103.1 Jukebox Radio, the Music You Remember.*** Big band, including '40s and '50s pop music, including Sid Mark Saturday evenings. Also, northern New Jersey news and old-time radio shows 9-10 Saturday mornings. All this worldwide action is from a surprisingly popular station whose nominal main FM site emits a fleapowered 0.0345 kW! However, the legitimacy of that FM operation is currently being challeneged by lawyers for WVNJ, a nearby competing station, so who knows what the end result will be. URL: http://www.audionet.com/radio/classics/wjux/. E-mail: jukeboxradio@aol.com.

Long Branch

RA288 mono **RA44** **WZVU Oldies 107.1.** Oldies, on-demand and live. URL: http://www.oldies107.com/index.htm. E-mail: (station) wzvu@oldies107.com; (Webmaster) webmaster@teconline.com.

West Caldwell

RA288 mono **WDHA 105.5 Jersey's Rock Radio.** New and classic rock. URL: (click on guitar in middle of page) http://www.wdhafm.com/. E-mail: (general) feedback@wdhafm.com; (Webmaster) webmaster@wdhafm.com.

New Mexico

Albuquerque

RA288 mono **KNKT 107.1 The Connection**, Armijo. Christian popular music and news from Pure Vision Ministries. URL: http://www.thegospel.com/cntidx.htm. E-mail: bruce@thegospel.com.

New York
(Also, see New Jersey)

Albany . . . and beyond

RA44 **WAMC Northeast Public Radio.** News and talk from the flagship station of the Northeast Public Radio network, which is affiliated with NPR and PRI. However, oddly enough, this station is aired over Web radio *on Fridays only*. URL: http://www.wamc.org/ or http://www.audionet.com/pub/wamc/. E-mail: wamc@transit.nyser.net. Toll-free phone (U.S. only): (800) 323-9292.

Buffalo

RA44 **WGR News Radio 55.** News, weather and sports, including coverage of the Buffalo Sabres hockey and Buffalo Bisons baseball teams, from Snow City USA. URL: http://www.wgr55.buffalo.net/, http://ns1.moran.com/htmld/wgr55/, http://www.audionet.com/radio/sports/wgr/ or http://www.1starnet.com/services/radio/starnetaudio.html. E-mail: wgr55@wgr55.com.

New York City

RA44 **ABC RadioNet.** The latest on-demand New York sports, weather, traffic and entertaining commentary, but (incredibly!) no news, from ABC's New York headquarters—not WABC. URL: http://www.abcradionet.com/newyork.htm. E-mail: abcquest@abc.com or newsabc@aol.com.

Coach K Official Site©

Duke University sports are covered exceptionally well on Web radio. Coach Mike Krzyzewski has helped mold Duke basketball into an international legend.

StreamWorks 1.0 **WBBR *Bloomberg News Radio.*** Bloomberg's widely respected financial, economic and general news coverage and talk is now available worldwide direct from the world's center of finance. Unfortunately, its audio via StreamWorks leaves something to be desired, with "hiccups" that always seem to come just as they're saying something you want to hear. However, *tempus fugit*, and in time this will surely be sorted out. In the meantime, try tuning in nights and weekends when the Web is least active and audio quality thus is best. URL: http://www.bloomberg.com/wbbr/. E-mail: feedback@bloomberg.com or http://www.bloomberg.com/feedback.html.

RA28.8 mono **WCBS *Newsradio 88.*** On-demand "Bootcamp" computer/technology program, along with various promos and other brief clips. Not an iota of news, live or otherwise, from this flagship station of CBS News! URL: http://www.pulver.com/wcbs.html. E-mail: (general) editor@wcbs88.com; (Bootcamp) http://www.pulver.com/bootcamp/feedback.html.

RA14.4 **WOR *Radio 710.*** News, talk and sports from New York City's #1 rated AM station, along with plenty of controversy from such personalities as the politically incorrect Bob Grant. Rutgers University sports, too. If you want to call in to a live talk show (1-212/391-2800), say you're listening on AudioNet and you'll be put at the front of the line. The WOR Web site is not the most reliable to download, so be patient and keep trying. URL: http://www.wor710.com/ or http://www.audionet.com/radio/talk/wor/. E-mail: wor@audionet.com.

Rochester

RA14.4 **WBER *90.5 FM*,** Henrietta. Alternative rock for parts of upstate New York. URL: http://wber.monroe.edu/.

Syracuse

WSYR *Voice of the Orange.* Award-winning news and live Syracuse University sports, as well as detailed reports on Syracuse's most important wintertime topic, the weather. URL: http://www.sybercuse.wsyr/ or http://www.audionet.com/radio/talk/wsyr/. E-mail: newcity@sybercuse.com.

North Carolina

Statewide

North Carolina High School Football. Weekly live football game, available afterward taped, along with on-demand reports on scores throughout the state's eight high-school sports districts. URL: http://www.capitolnet.com/hs-football/. E-mail: george_habel@cbcnet.interpath.net.

North Carolina News Network, Raleigh. On-demand statewide news and news headlines, sports reports and weather, with strongest coverage Monday through Friday. URL: http://www.capitolnet.com/ncnn/. E-mail: matt_willoughby@cbcnet.interpath.net.

Local

Charlotte

Carolina Panthers Radio Network. Live and taped Panthers football games, as well as other information, on-demand, about the progress of the team. Also, see

From this unusual building comes Syracuse University sports, as well as award-winning news and weather from shivery upstate New York.

WRAL-TV5, below. URL: http://www.capitolnet.com/panthers/. E-mail: george_habel@cbcnet.interpath.net.

WRFX 99.7. Recent classic rock. URL: http://www.wrfx.com/ or http://www.audionet.com/radio/classicrock/wrfx/.

Hickory

mono **WXRC *95dot7 Deep Cuts.*** Classic rock. URL: http://www.audionet.com/radio/album/wxrc/. E-mail: wxrc@audionet.com.

Raleigh-Durham-Chapel Hill Research Triangle

Duke Sports, Durham. Live and on-demand games of Duke University's Blue Devils football team, as well as a wide variety of on-demand feature programs about the team and other Duke athletic activities. Also, see **WRAL-TV5**, below. URL: (news and features, all Duke sports, plus live football games) http://www.dukesports.com/; (live and taped football games) http://www.goduke.com/cyber/cyber.html. E-mail: mcragg@acpub.duke.edu or bdw@interpath.com.

[RA44] North Carolina State University *Wolfpack Capitol Sports Network*, Raleigh. NCSU Wolfpack football games live and taped, along with reports on team activities. Also, see **WRAL-TV5**, below. URL: (games)

Kevin Broadcasting System

KOOL Vegas Radio's Jodi Lawrence studied at the University of Copenhagen before tossing her hat into the Las Vegas radio scene. A prolific writer, she's listed in the International Who's Who of Women.

http://www.capitolnet.com/ncsu/; (official 30-second wolf howl) http://www.agrafx.com/pack/fan. E-mail: bill@agrafx.com.

[RA44] WRAL-FM *Mix 101.5*, Raleigh. Rock and pop from the '70s, '80s and '90s, as well as news and sports, including Duke University and University of North Carolina football and basketball, along with Winston Cup events. URL: (audio) http://www.wralfm.com/sound.html, http://www.audionet.com/radio/news/wral/ or http://www.1starnet.com/services/radio/starnetaudio.html. E-mail: steve_reynolds@wralfm.com; (text) http://www.wralfm.com/.

[RA44] WRAL-TV 5. Live and on-demand TV audio of news, weather, sports scores and sports commentary, plus live games from North Carolina State, Duke University, the Carolina Panthers and the Durham Bulls. URL: (news) http://www.wral-tv.com/news/; (weather) http://www.wral-tv.com/weather/; (sports) http://www.wral-tv.com/sports/sportstalk.html. E-mail: http://www.wral-tv.com/feedback/email/.

[StreamWorks] 2.0 **WXYC *University of North Carolina***, Chapel Hill. Award-winning eclectic rock and talk in university environment. Also, separate live and on-demand Web radio coverage of Tar Heel sports. URL: (WXYC) http://sunsite.unc.edu/wxyc/index.html; (Tar Heel Sports) http://www.goheels.com/ontheair.html. E-mail: (WXYC, general) wxyz@unc.edu or rossti@email.unc.com; (WXYC Webmaster) shoffner@sunsite.unc.edu;

Star 100.7

No, this isn't next season's "Baywatch" cast. It's the tireless on-air staff of Star 100.7 in sunny San Diego, where you'd rather be if you'd rather not be in Philadelphia.

(Tar Heel Sports, general) chris@netscan.com; (Tar Heel Sports Webmaster) webmaster@internetsports.com.

Ohio

Ashtabula

RA288 mono **WKKY Country 104.7**, Geneva. Country hits, along with local news and weather. URL: (click on "WKKY On The Net") http://www.wkky.com/. E-mail: wkky@mwweb.com.

RA288 mono **WZOO 102 Zoo FM.** Light rock. URL: http://www.knownet.net/ wzoo.htm. E-mail: http://www.knownet.net/form.htm.

Cincinnati

RA288 mono **RA288** stereo **WGRR Oldies 103.5 FM.** Cheerful Sixties rock and pop offerings in a predictable package, live in mono with on-demand shows in stereo. Note that page downloads are Java-Jive slow. URL: http://www.wgrr1035.com/audio.htm. E-mail: (staff) http://www.wgrr1035.com/email.htm; (Webmaster) http://www.wgrr1035.com/webmastr.htm.

Columbus

RA288 mono **WCLT T-100**, Newark. Country. If you want to get an idea of where Web radio's country music fans hail from and what they think of it, check out WCLT's Wall of Fame at http://wclt.com/addguest.htm. URL: http://www.wclt.com/realaudio.htm. E-mail: http://wclt.com/email.htm or http://wclt.com/addguest.htm.

RA288 mono **WLVQ The Total Rock-n-Roll Experience.** Rock. URL: http://www.qfm96.com/home.html. E-mail: wlvq@cis.compuserve.com.

Dayton

RA44 **WGNZ Good News 1110 Gospel Radio**, Fairborn. Live Southern ("white") gospel music and Christian programs, plus USA Radio Network news. Also, an on-demand religious message. URL: http://www.good-news.org/. E-mail: (station) wgnz@good-news.org; (Webmaster) netmgr@coax.net.

RA44 **WTUE 104.7.** No live audio—tiptoe through the cybertulips—but some on-demand rock musical clips, news of the local rock scene and ABC news headlines, plus some live concerts. URL: http://www.arsdayton.com/wtue.html. E-mail: wtue@erinet.com.

Kent

StreamWorks 2.0 **WKSU Kent State University.** Classical music, plus local and university news both live and on-demand. However, because of rights issues, for now their non-local programming is not being aired over the Web. URL: http://www.wksu.kent.edu/. E-mail: letters@wksu.kent.edu or http://www.wksu.kent.edu/guestbook.

Oklahoma
Statewide

RA288 mono **KTRT Oklahoma Radio Network**, Tulsa. News, talk and sports, including live baseball.

This bumper sticker is from KBIX, part of the statewide Oklahoma Radio Network. Expat Okies and Rush Limbaugh fans can ogle stickers like this at http://www.ktrt.com/bumper.html.

URL: http://www.ktrt.com/ or http://www.audionet.com/radio/talk/ktrt/. E-mail: (general) rreed@ktrt.com; (Webmaster) silver@tulsawalk.com. Toll-free phone (U.S. only): (888) 439-3733.

Local

Tulsa-Muskogee

 mono **KHTT K·HITS 106.9 FM.** Contemporary hit radio, plus local news. URL: http://khits.com/. E-mail: (general) info@khits.com; (news) katrina@khits.com.

KWMJ TV53 Oral Roberts University. Inspiration programming, along with such entertainment as Ozzie and Harriet, live from Oral Roberts University's TV outlet. URL: http://tv53.oru.edu/kwmj.html. E-mail: hsalem@oru.edu. Toll-free phone (U.S. only): (800) 678-8876.

Oregon

Portland

KBNP AM 1410 Business Radio. Whether you're in Portland, Oregon, or Portland, Maine, you can tune in for the latest financial and personal news from various sources, including the Bloomberg and Business News networks. URL: http://www.kbnp.com/ or http://www.audionet.com/radio/business/kbnp/. E-mail: kbnp@kbnp.com.

KFXX The Fan. Sports. URL: http://www.kfxx.com/ or http://www.audionet.com/radio/sports/kfxx/. E-mail: lshannon@kfxx.com.

Karen Mills is the music director for Columbus, Ohio's country music station, WCLT-FM. Karen is into sports, long walks, movies and "anything else you can throw my way." You can hear her weekday evenings, or contact her direct by e-mail.

mono **KGON Classic Rock 92.3.** Classic Rock (how'd you guess?). URL: http://www.kgon.com/ or http://www.audionet.com/radio/classicrock/kgon/. E-mail: lshannon@kgon.com.

KNRK New Rock Revolution. Alternative rock. URL: http://www.knrk.com/ or http://www.audionet.com/radio/alternative/knrk/. E-mail: (general) tbaker@knrk.com; (requests) request@knrk.com.

Pennsylvania

Allentown

mono **WALN Cableradio FM 92 (proposed).** On-demand polkas, doo wop and other oldies music from the Fifties and Sixties which are also aired over world band station WWCR in Nashville. URL: http://www.clevelandstyle.com/waln.

You think *you* have an identity crisis? Try being a fox...on a surfboard...wearing boots and funny pants while listening to country music. Only in California, and you can hear it all live and in RealAudio over KZLA, Los Angeles.

E-mail: 02404.3250@compuserve.com or walncable@cis.compuserve.com.

Philadelphia

Also see **WKXW/WBBS New Jersey 101.5**, above, in the New Jersey section. **RA288** mono **WPLY 100.3 FM Y100 Philadelphia's New Rock**, Media. Today's rock. URL: http:// www.y100.com/. E-mail: (station) chucktisa@aol.com; (Webmaster) webmaster@y100.com. Toll-free phone (U.S. only): (800) 232-1003.

Philipsburg

RA288 mono **RA144** **WUBZ The Buzz 105.9 FM.** Alternative rock—retro and new wave—live and on-demand from a small town in the hinterland of

Pennsylvania's former coal-mining country. Young station (just bought out), young staff, young music . . . and very Internet-aware ("the campus" is virtual). The occasional technical hiccups at this site should be ironed out by the time you read this. URL: http:// www.thecampus.com/ra/wubz/ index.html. E-mail: buzz@thecampus.com.

Pittsburgh

RA288 mono **WRRK 96.9 FM.** Excellent classic rock—about as good a playlist as you're likely to find these days on the Web or over the air—although most jocks, promos and ads are as predictable as cheeseburgers. Songs are mostly from the Sixties and

Seventies, along with some blues and later stuff. If and when they go to Real Audio 28.8 stereo, this will be a worldwide listening treat to console boomers squinting at PC monitors through Varilux lenses. URL: http://www.rrk.com/, http://www.audionet.com/radio/classicrock/wrrk/ or http://www.1starnet.com/services/radio/starnetaudio.html. E-mail: quinn@sgi.net or http://www.rrk.com/feedback.html.

(RA44) WTAE 1250 *Talk Radio*. Sports talk from the official station for the Pittsburgh Steelers, Pittsburgh Penguins and Pittsburgh Panthers. URL: http://audionet.com/radio/sports.wtae/ or http://www.wtaeradio.com/. E-mail: (general) bgilbert@hearst.com; (Webmaster) readams@hearst.com.

State College

(RA44) Penn State University. Nittany Lions football live. URL: http://www.sportsline.com/u/radio/live/pennst.htm. E-mail: (University) sports@www.psu.edu or www@www.psu.edu; (RealAudio Webmaster) genqandc@sportsline.com.

Rhode Island

Providence

(RA288) stereo WBRU 95.5 *BRU*. Alternative rock, mostly, from this deservedly award-winning station—three years in a trot it's been the Rolling Stone Radio Station of the Year. But there's more: R&B/hip-hop/gospel Sunday evenings, followed by reggae into the wee hours. Other non-rock insomniac offerings are blues on Mondays and jazz on Tuesdays and Wednesdays. URL: (click on the ear) http://wbru.com/. E-mail: http://wbru.com/feedback.html.

Tennessee

Memphis

(RA288) mono WEGR *Rock 103*. Rock, plus a blues show Sunday night. URL: http://www.rock103.com/ or http://www.audionet.com/radio/classicrock/wegr. E-mail: wegr103@aol.com.

(RA44) WHBQ *Sports 56*. Sports talk, along with live coverage of Memphis Riverkings CHL games. URL: http://www.audionet.com/radio/sports/whbq/ or http://www.flinn.com/56.html. E-mail: flinn@basenet.net, placing "WHBQ" in the subject line. Toll-free phone (U.S. only): (888) 360-8255.

(RA288) mono WRVR *The River*. Adult contemporary. If you e-mail the station, you get a free CD, no matter where in the world you live. URL: http://www.audionet.com/radio/contemporary/wrvr/. E-mail: wrvr@audionet.com.

(RA288) mono Internet Wave WRXQ *96X*. Alternative rock, live and with on-demand musical and program selections. URL: (live and on-demand) http://www.96x.com/; (live) http://www.audionet.com/radio/alternative/wrxq/. E-mail: (Backstage Wall) http://www.96x.com/addguest.html.

Country music star Ty England visits KLLL in Lubbock, Texas. England is a former Oklahoma college roommate of Garth Brooks, who helped him launch his singing career.

Nashville

RA288 mono **WRLT Lightning 100.** Adult album alternative format. This station's audio has been balky—don't be surprised if all you get is silence—but things may have improved by the time you read this. URL: http://www.audionet.com/ or http://wrlt.com/. E-mail: http://198.79.88.14/wrlt/listen.htm or wrlt@audionet.com.

Texas

Austin

RA288 mono **KGSR Radio Austin**, Bastrop. Adult album alternative.

URL: http://www.kgsr.com/ or http://www.audionet.com/radio/album/kgsr/. **RA288** mono **KROX New Rock Alternative.** Alternative rock. URL: http://www.audionet.com/radio/alternative/krox/.

Beaumont

RA288 mono **KKMY Classic 104.5.** Hot adult contemporary. URL: http://www.kkmy.com or http://www.audionet.com/radio/. E-mail: kkmy@kkmy.com. Toll-free phone (U.S. only): (800) 330-5569 or (800) 329-9595.

RA288 mono **KLVI AM 560.** News and talk. URL: http://www.klvi.com/ or http://www.audionet.com/radio/. E-mail: klvi@klvi.com. Toll-free phone (U.S. only): (800) 330-5584 or (800) 329-9595.

RA288 mono **KYKR K95.1.** Country. URL: http://www.kykr.com or http://www.audionet.com/radio/. E-mail: kykr@kykr.com. Toll-free phone (U.S. only): (800) 330-5957 or (800) 329-9595.

College Station-Bryan

RA44 **WTAW 1150 AM.** Sports talk and news from the station that airs play-by-play coverage of not only Aggies games, but also Longhorn contests. (If you think we're talking about marbles and cattle, forget this station.) URL: (station, including Aggies sports) http://www.audionet.com/radio/sports/wtaw/ or http://www.wtaw.com/menu.htm; (Aggies sports only) http://www.audionet.com/schools/tamu/. E-mail: radio@wtaw.com.

Dallas-Ft. Worth

RA288 mono **KAAM 620 Unforgettable**, Plano. Pop and classics from the past 50 years. URL: http://www.audionet.com/radio/classics/kaam/. E-mail: kaam@audionet.com.

RA288 mono **KDGE 94.5 The Edge.** Alternative rock, including cuts from the Eighties. URL: http://www.kdge.com/kdge/ or http://www.audionet.com/radio/alternative/kdge/. E-mail: merrittc@airmail.net.

RA288 mono **KKDA K104**, Grand Prairie. Urban contemporary/soul. URL: http://www2.k104.com/k104.html, http://www.audionet.com/ or http://www.naomi.com/kkda.htm. E-mail: rolandmar@aol.com.

RA44 **KLIF 570 AM The Talk Team.** Sports, talk and news. It's also AudioNet's flagship station, which may be why its audio quality is relatively good even at 14.4 kb. URL: http://www.klif.com/, http://www.audionet.com/radio/talk/klif/

Amerinet

For the latest on UFOs, New World Order activity, BATF actions or black helicopters overhead, tune in Jeffery Bakers' "Baker Report" over KDNO in Delano, California.

or http://www.1starnet.com/services/ radio/starnetaudio.html. E-mail: klif-db@ix.netcom.com, http:// www.klif.com/mailroom.html or klif@audionet.com. Toll-free talkline: (800) 583-1570—tell them you're listening on AudioNet, and you'll be the next to go on the air.

RA288 mono **KPLX 99.5 *Flex Your Plex.*** Gen-yew-wine country music from Dallis Texis, along with NASCAR reports. With a program director called "Smokey Rivers," this station just has to be a bit of paradise for would-be Bubbas from Yuma to Yurp. URL: http://www.kplx.com/, http:// www.audionet.com/pub/kplx/kplx.com or http://www.1starnet.com/services/ radio/starnetaudio.html. E-mail: onairinc@ix.netcom.com. Toll-free request line (U.S. only): (800) 999-5759—say you're listening to AudioNet, and you go on next.

RA288 mono **KRNB 105.7 *Classic R-n-B.*** Worth hearing for a different twist on the black musical

experience. URL: http:// www.audionet.com/radio/urban/krnb/.

RA288 mono **KRSM *The Zone* 93.3 FM.** Adult album alternative. URL: http:// www.audionet.com/radio/album/ thezone/. E-mail: zone@audionet.com.

RA288 mono **KSKY *Christian AM 660*,** Balch Springs. Christian programming, including Southern gospel music. URL: http://www.ksky.com/ or http://www.audionet.com/radio/ christian/ksky/. R-mail: kskyradio@aol.com.

RA44 **KTCK *The Ticket.*** Sports talk. URL: http://www.theticket.com/ or http://www.audionet.com/radio/sports/ ktck/. E-mail: princess@theticket.com.

RA44 **KTVT-TV *Channel 11.*** Live and on-demand audio of local TV newscasts five times each weekday, including sports and weather coverage, plus a few newscasts over the weekend. URL: http://www.ktvt.com/ index.html or http:// www.audionet.com/ radio/tv/ktvt/. E-mail: ktvt@ktvt.com.

Back when it was called hillbilly music and Johnny Cash still had his voice, folks in Dallas wanted no part of C&W. Now it's called country music, and legions in Big D's urban canyons soak it up over popular KPLX.

RA288 mono **KZPS Classic Rock Station.** Classic rock from the '60s, '70s and '80s. URL: http://kzps.com/kzps/ or http://www.audionet.com/radio/classicrock/kzps/. E-mail: (general) brenda@ontheair.com; (DJ Kacy Harrison) kaceh@airmail.net.

Houston

RA44 **KHCB 105.7 FM.** Predictable Christian evangelical local and network programming, such as Billy Graham. Includes inspirational music, which sometimes sounds dreadful over this Web link. Interestingly, given the Web's worldwide reach, their sister station KHCB-AM in Galveston, which broadcasts in Chinese, Vietnamese and Spanish, is not on Web radio. URL: http://www.khcb.org/. E-mail: khcb@nol.net.

RA288 mono **KRBE 104 FM.** Top 40 pop, including occasional live concerts by Lisa Loeb, Susanna Hoffs and others. URL: http://www.krbe.com/ or http://www.audionet.com/radio/top40pop/krbe/. E-mail: mailbox@krbe.com.

RA288 mono **KTBZ The Buzz.** Alternative rock. URL: http://www.thebuzz.com/ or http://www.audionet.com/radio/alternative/ktbz/. E-mail: thebuzz@thebuzz.com.

Lubbock

RA288 mono **KLLL Hot Country 96.3.** Since 1958, KLLL has been airing country music from the Texas Panhandle, where Texas and Oklahoma traditions of country music have long fermented, like good whiskey. If you

Houston's Katrina Tyler made it to Tulsa's KHTT, where she's news director, by first apprenticing at a station in Alaska. As a child, she got her interest in radio by listening to KRBE in Houston. Now, both KRBE and KHTT entertain the world over Web radio.

want to see what other Web radio listeners have to say about KLLL, their guestbook is at http://www.klll.com/djguest.html. URL: http://www.klll.com/. E-mail: http://www.klll.com/addguest.html.

Paris

RA288 mono **KOYN Your Country 93.9.** Country music, with live audio and some on-demand music clips. URL: http://www.1starnet.com/clients/koyn/koyn.html, http://www.audionet.com/radio/country/koyn/ or http://www.1starnet.com/services/radio/

StarNet

Wade White's songs can be enjoyed over the air, as well as on-demand, over KOYN in Paris, Texas. KOYN is a hoe-down favorite among Web radio's many country music fans.

starnetaudio.html. E-mail: koyn@stargate.1starnet.com.

San Antonio

RA44 **Air Force Radio News.** Just that, from Brooks AFB's Human Systems Center. A five-minute newscast is updated and on-demand each weekday afternoon at 3:00 PM Central Time. URL: http://www.brooks.af.mil/realaudio/newsbyte.html. E-mail: bill.stephenson@platinum.brooks.af.mil.
RA288 mono **KSJL 96.1 FM.** Urban contemporary/soul. URL: http://

www.ksjl.com/default.html or http://www.audionet.com/radio/urban/ksjl/. E-mail: jockbox@ksjl.com. Toll-free phone (U.S. only): (800) 460-5755.
RA44 **WOAI AM 1200.** News, talk and sports talk. WOAI was once a great clear-channel powerhouse, booming in to listeners throughout much of the United States and Mexico. But in the early Fifties, just as television was changing the face of radio, a World War II vintage bomber crashed into the station's elaborate antenna towers. They were replaced with lesser stuff, and WOAI settled back to become just another local station. Now, thanks to Web radio, WOAI's voice— the first on the Web from San Antonio—is once again audible from afar, even though during the weeks before we went to press that voice was being degraded by a consistent and annoying audio buzz. URL: http://www.woai.com/, http://www.audionet.com/radio/talk/woai/ or http://www.1starnet.com/services/radio/starnetaudio.html. E-mail: progers@woai.com.

Winfield-Mt. Pleasant

RA288 mono **KALK K-LAKE 97.7 FM.** Mix of pop and soft rock. URL: (RealAudio) http://206.103.100.4/clients/klake/livefeed.html, http://www.audionet.com/radio/mix/klake/ or http://www.1starnet.com/services/radio/starnetaudio.html; (text and RealAudio) http://www.1starnet.com/clients/klake/klake.html. E-mail: klake@stargate.1starnet.com.

Utah

Salt Lake City

RA44 **KFAN SportsTalk 1320.** News and sports talk from the station which just replaced the former KCRN. URL: http://www.audionet.com/radio/sports/kfan/.

StreamWorks 2.0 **KSL 1160 Newsradio.** News, sports, traffic, weather and talk from this CBS affiliate station. URL: http://www.ksl.com/radio/. E-mail: peterparker@ksl.com.

Virginia

Chesapeake Bay

RA288 stereo **WNVZ 104.5 FM Z104 Today's Best Music**, Norfolk. Today's rock and hip-hop hits. URL: http://www.z104.com/ or http://www.z104.com/index.html. E-mail: sean@z104.com.

West Virginia

Charleston

See **WOWK**, **Huntington**, which has studios in Charleston.

Huntington

RA44 **WOWK TV 13.** This CBS affiliate has just installed RealAudio, but currently airs only the weather forecast, on-demand. The station plans for this to expand, probably in 1997, to include "the newscasts, if not more." URL: http://www.ramlink.net/wowk/. E-mail: (station) wowk@ramlink.net; (Webmaster) edge@ramlink.net.

Keyser

RA288 mono **WQZK-FM Q94.** This mountain-top station airs mostly classic rock, with occasional forays into today's rock, offering audio clips only a deejay's mother could love. It's live, too, but *only* if you use Netscape. Indeed, this appears to be the only Web radio station in existence that won't provide audio via Internet Explorer 3.x! URL: (clips) http://www.wqzk.com/; (live, but only with Netscape) http://www.wqzk.com/livepanl.htm. E-mail: (station) homepagecomments@wqzk.com; (Webmaster) wqzk@.miworld.net.

Washington State

Seattle

RA288 v3.0 mono **KING Classic KING FM.** A golden strand in the Web! Outstanding recorded and live orchestral, chamber and other classical music, along with live airings from the Seattle Opera. This award-winning station's profits are parceled out among the Seattle Symphony, Seattle Opera and Corporate Council for the Arts. Ads and promos? Yes, but they're relatively few and non-intrusive. In RealAudio 3.0—nominally in stereo via ISBN or better, but mono on 28.8 kb or less—it sounds as good as any other station on the Web as of when we went to press, albeit with some echo and the odd "hiccup," both characteristic of beta v3.0. (For now, you can compare KING's audio with that of the RealAudio v2.0 classical music

"Nudestock" fans of Seattle's Rock 99.9 get together cheek to cheek to spell out the station's call letters.

channel of SW Network at http://swnetworks.com/cgi-bin/Webdriver?M1val=realaudio.htm). URL: http://www.king.org/. E-mail: mailbox@king.org.

RA288 mono **RA44** *KISW Rock 99.9 FM.* On-demand comedy, features and rock clips. No live audio thus far, but they hope to go this route shortly. URL: http://www.kisw.com. E-mail: (general) kisswmd@kisw.com; (Webmaster) jmoss@hotlink.net or webmaster@kisw.com.

RA288 mono **RA44** *KMTT The Mountain 103.7 FM.* On-demand rock music and chat, but no live offering. URL: http://www.kmtt.com/ra/. E-mail: (general) mountain@kmtt.com; (Webmaster) richm@metawave.com or http://www.kmtt.com/interact/messages/9696.html.

Olympia

RA44 *TVW Washington State's Public Affairs Network.* TV audio, mostly on-demand, of Washington State official proceedings—think of it as "the C-Span of Washington State." With such scintillating offerings as "House Finance Committee Holds a Meeting to Discuss Revenue Forecast," this station is definitely an acquired taste. Equally, this sort of narrowcasting is also one of Web radio's theoretical virtues, so tune in and test the theory. URL: http://www.tvw.org/newra.htm. E-mail: tvw@tvw.org.

Wisconsin

Antigo
🔊 **WRLO 105.3 Northern Wisconsin's Sports Connection.** On-demand daily comments from the Green Bay Packers' Head Coach, but nothing more. URL: http://unix.newnorth.net/wrlo/packers.htm. E-mail: wrlo@newnorth.net. Toll-free phone (U.S. and Canada only): (800) 261-9756.

NATIONAL AND INTERNATIONAL

🔊 **ABC Radio News.** Not just the hourly news, but all kinds of fresh on-demand audio from much of the nightly ABC-TV World News Tonight to David Brinkley. This is a well-thought-out site that puts those of the other major American networks to shame. Check it out. URL: http://www.abcradionet.com/.
🔊 **Air Force Radio News**—see **San Antonio, Texas**.
🔊 **American Independent Network.** Live TV audio. URL and E-mail: http://www.audionet.com/radio/tv/ain/.
🔊 **AudioNet College Sports.** Fifty or so college and university sports teams are broadcast

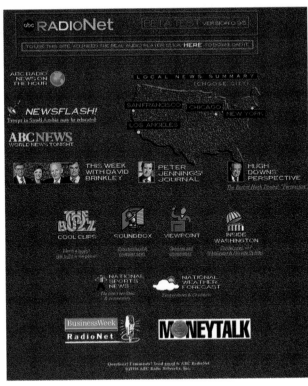

ABC Radio News has the best Web radio site of any of the major American networks.

Houston's "Buzz 107.5" brings alternative rock to Xers worldwide.

live over AudioNet College Sports, the "ESPN of the Web." This site is a godsend for college sports buffs whose favorite teams don't have their own independent Web radio operations. However, even for those that do, the tie-in with AudioNet is a major advantage, as AudioNet's high-volume server configuration can better handle the huge listening spikes found during sports events. URL: http://www.audionet.com/schools/. E-mail: bjacoby@audionet.com.

RA288 RA44 **AudioNet THE Broadcast Network on the Internet.** This is the primary hyperlink for Web radio, but it's much more, with lots of helpful features and extras. An increasing proportion of North American stations coming on for the first time with Web radio are affiliates of AudioNet, so this is the best place in cyberspace to keep up with changes. URL (page down three times or so for new sites):

http://www.audionet.com/radio/. E-mail: (public relations) lboyd@audionet.com; (administration) mcuban@audionet.com.

StreamWorks 1.0 **Bloomberg Information News**—see **New York City**.

RA44 **Brownfield Network Audio Farm News Reports.** Livestock, grain and other farm and ranch news individualized for stations in 1) Nebraska, 2) Iowa, 3) Missouri, 4) Illinois and 5) Indiana. URL: http://www.agnews.com/news.html. E-mail: info@agnews.com.

RA288 mono **Cable Radio Network CRN The Radio Channel.** News, sports, talk and adult contemporary music that's fed to U.S. cable-TV systems in over 16 states. URL: http://www.audionet.com/radio/contemporary/crn/. E-mail: crnradio@aol.com.

RA288 mono **RA44** **CBS News Up to the Minute.** Various on-demand clips of news and features. Much smoke and little fire, but it's still better than CBS Radio's offerings, below. URL: http://uttm.com/. E-mail: mail@uttm.com.

RA44 CBS Radio Networks Online. Some on-demand airings of such features as the Mary Matalin Show, along with clips from recent NFL and other games. You can almost hear the muttering upstairs at Black Rock, "We'd better not put anything on the Web live, or we'll tick off the affiliates." Withal, a dismal showing for one of the world's premiere broadcasting organizations. URL: http://www.cbsradio.com/. E-mail: crnwebmaster@cbs.com.

RA44 CBS Radio Sports Online. One or two on-demand NFL highlights. URL: http://www.realaudio.com/contentp/rabest/cbsnfl.html. E-mail: nfl@cbs.com.

RA44 CIRnet. Christian radio network with music and sermons. URL: http://cirnet.com/. E-mail: info@cirnet.com.

StreamWorks 2.0 College Radio Network. Commercial programs fed to affiliated college stations throughout the United States. URL: http://www.internetwork.com/crn/crn.htm. E-mail: crnetwork@aol.com or http://www.interwork.com/crn/infoform.htm.

RA288 mono Court TV News. Live from the courtrooms of America is cable TV's popular Court TV. If you're at work or somewhere else where this can't be picked up in the usual way, you can still get its live audio of court proceedings, often of juicy trials that tabloid news. That's only when it's on, of course, which usually is weekdays—or at least some weekdays. URL: http://www.courttv.com/live/. E-mail: http://www.courttv.com/contact/.

RA44 C-Span—see **District of Columbia**.

RA44 Drivetime The Golf Radio Show. On-demand news and interviews from this Monday-Friday 3 minute network show

You don't have to walk a mile to hear Phoenix's "Camel 108." It's one in a growing roster of country music stations on Web radio.

Small town, big voice. From the outback of northeast Texas to the ears of the world comes gentle music from K-LAKE, located in a town that's barely a speck on the map.

for golf aficionados. URL: http://golf.capitolnet.com/. E-mail: http://golf.capitolnet.com/comments.html or http://golf.capitolnet.com/ask.html.

RA44 **ESPN Radio Network.** Live coverage of NFL football and NBA basketball games, plus on-demand audio from The Fabulous Sports Babe, SportsBeat, Radio Weekend, NFL on ESPN and other offerings. URL: http://www.espnet.sportszone.com/editors/liveaudio/index.html. E-mail: (general) szletters@starwave.com, espnet1@espn.com, http://espnet.sportszone.com/subscriber/letters.html, http://espnet.sportszone.com/subscriber/espn-let.html or http://

espnet.sportszone.com/subscriber/contact.html; (questions to announcers) http://espnet.sportszone.com/editors/talk/qa/questions/radio.html; (Fabulous Sports Babe) http://espnet.com/editors/talk/qa/questions/dababe.html; (opinion poll) http://espnet.sportszone.com/editors/talk/polls.html.

RA288 mono **RA44** **FOX News Channel.** Live TV audio, day and night, from the Fox News Channel. Included are news, news analysis, personal help, financial news and a wide range of features. In all, a solid, down-to-earth Web radio showing—after all, what sense is Web radio for a news operation if it doesn't offer a live feed?

Other news-oriented networks with snazzy sites having no live audio would do well to follow Fox's precedent. URL: (click on either the 28.8 or 14.4 ear at the bottom of the Web page) http://www.foxnews.com/channel/listen.sml. E-mail: comments@foxnews.com or scott@foxnews.com.

Michael Reagan Talk Show. Ronald Reagan's son discusses various topics of interest to political conservatives. Live and on-demand, with file-downloaded excerpts from The Gipper's speeches also available on-demand. URL: (Michael Reagan Show) http://www.audionet.com/shows/reagan/ or http://204.58.152.70/pub/reagan/audionet.html; (Ronald Reagan audio clips) http://www.reagan.com/mf.main/ronald/audio.html. E-mail: http://www.webforums.com/forums/trace/host/msa21.html. For more audio offerings along these philosophical lines, try the Cato Institute at http://www.cato.org.

Monitor Radio (when operating). Planned new service with audio from the Christian Science Monitor's feed to PRI affiliates. URL: http://town.hall.org/radio/Monitor/feeds.html. E-mail: (general) radio@csps.com; (letters and reception reports) letterbox@csms.com. Toll-free phone (U.S. only): (800) 288-7090.

National Public Radio. Freshly updated on-demand audio news, news analysis and features from NPR. URL: (general, streamed) http://www.npr.org/index.html; (general, streamed or file download) http://www.wrn.org/stations/npr.html; ("Car Talk" on-demand audio clips) http://cartalk.com/Radio/replay.html. E-mail: (general) www-info@npr.org; (specific shows) http://www.npr.org/e-mail.html; ("Car Talk") http://cartalk.com/Tools/feedback.pl.

National Religious Broadcasters Involved Christian Radio Network. A variety of on-demand Christian programs from Chuck Colson and others. URL: http://www.icrn.com/. E-mail: icrninfo@thedomaingroup.com.

NBC Nightly News. Somebody at the Peacock—not to mention Microsoft—spent beaucoup bucks

Radio Sedaye Iran services the large expatraite community of Iranians in Southern California and, now, the world.

for NBC and MSNBC Web sites full of attractive pages, but with only a smattering of audio clips to satisfy the growing legions of Web radio listeners. Withal, the pages with audio related to the NBC Nightly News contain real news, not fluff, and the audio quality is up to snuff. URL: http://www.msnbc.com/onair/nbc/nightlynews/default.asp. E-mail: nightly@msnbc.com.

RA44 **ToolVox New World Chronicle/USAID.** Archive of weekly on-demand half-hour reports from the United States Agency for International Development (USAID). Boring presentation, but where else can you hear Hillary Clinton discussing Batman and Superman comics that educate Bosnian children about land mines? URL: http://www.info.usaid.gov/press/nwc/. E-mail: pinquiries@usaid.gov.

RA44 **StreamWorks** 1.0 **NFL Players Inc Radio.** On-demand NFL commentary, prepared by football mavens at **Fox** (see) and **WTEM** (see Maryland). URL: http://www.sportsline.com/u/nflpa/nflradio.html. E-mail: (general) genqandc@sportsline.com; (bulletin board) http://www.sportsline.com/u/chat/chats/nflpa/chat.cgi; (Webmaster) techsupport@sportsline.com.

RA288 mono **RA44** **Premiere Radio Networks.** On-demand audio clips of comedy, celebs and commentary. Their Web site may still be advertising Trojan condom screen savers. (Don't even *think* of asking how they're installed.) URL: http:// www.premrad.com/. E-mail: (general) ecanale@premrad.com; (Webmaster) webmaster@premrad.com.

RA44 **Prime Sports Radio Network** *Fox Sports Direct.* Sports talk and game coverage from around the country. URL: http://libertysports.com/radio.htm or http:// www.audionet.com/radio/sports/psr/. E-mail: webmaster@libertysports.com. Toll-free phone (U.S. only): (800) 305-3993.

RA288 **Radio Free Asia.** Funded by the American government, but officially "not an official voice of the United States Government," RFA plans to provide on-demand news

XTRA

Popular sports commentator Jim Rome is heard worldwide over XTRA AM-690 in San Diego/Tijuana.

and features in Burmese, Cambodian (Khmer), Korean, Laotian, Mandarin (Standard Chinese), Tibetan and Vietnamese. URL: http://www.rfa.org/.

RA44 **Radio Reading Services**, Lawrence, Kansas. Gobs of printed materials—the list is enormous, and includes everything from newspapers to antiques—are read on-demand for free by first-rate readers. Nominally this is for blind people, but it makes for great background listening for anybody who's tickling the ivories on a PC. Presented by In Touch Networks and the Kansas Audio-Reader Network. URL: http://www.tstradio.com/intouch.html. E-mail: tstinfo@tstradio.com.

RA288 stereo **RA288** mono **RA44** **RealAudio Audio on Demand for the Internet.** AudioNet is the primary hyperlink for Web radio, but Progressive Technology's RealAudio site is the main hyperlink for the broader field of Internet audio. Its Timecast feature allows for mass customization, if you are so inclined, which lets you program what you want to hear, when. A high proportion of Web radio stations currently use RealAudio. URL: (general) http://www.realaudio.com or http://www.prognet.com; (new sites) http://www.timecast.com/new_site.html. E-mail: http://www.christie.prognet.com/support/comments.html.

RA288 mono **Reel Top 40 Radio Repository.** Veteran DJ Uncle Ricky presents on-demand 1959-1986 clips of DJ chatter from top-40 stations throughout the United States. Great nostalgia—too bad more Web radio sites don't have their own elder archives available on their Web sites to help cement listener loyalty. URL: http://www.reelradio.com/. E-mail: ricky@sna.com.

RA288 **RFE-RL**—see **Czech Republic**.

RA44 **SIM Missionary Radio.** On-demand Christian talks aired on radio stations throughout North America. URL: http://www.sim.org/radio/index.html. E-mail: radio@sim.org.

RA288 stereo **Spin College Radio.** On-demand replays of this nationally syndicated alternative rock show. URL: http://www.premrad.com/music/spin/spin.html. E-mail: webmaster@premrad.com.

RA44 **StreamWorks** 1.0 **SportsLine USA.** Live and archived Web radio sports talk and games. URL: http://www.sportsline.com/u/radio/live.index.html. E-mail: genqandc@sportsline.com. Toll-free phone (U.S. only): (800) 806-9308.

StreamWorks **The Cutting Edge of Digital Audio and Video.** The definitive hyperlink to **StreamWorks** sites, including the relatively small number used for Web radio. With enough bandwidth, **StreamWorks** is hard to beat. But in the real

Polls consistly show that country music is just about America's favorite, but you'd never know it from the relatively small number of AM/FM country stations. Web radio helps overcome this and also reaches fans in other countries.

world of 28.8 kb modems and Internet congestion, it "hiccups" badly, disconnects without warning, and lacks even the most basic of operating features. This might be okay were the company moving in the right direction, but instead it seems to be Gearhead City, with little understanding of the real world needs of listeners who aren't, like them, advanced software experts. Still, **StreamWorks** remains free to listeners, so do a rain dance and hope for the best. URL: http://www.streamworks.com/ or http://www.xingtech.com/.

StreamWorks 2.0 **Talk America Radio Network.** Some 40-odd talk shows, some odder than others, ranging from Bo Gritz' "Freedom Calls" to various health offerings, with Chuck Harder (formerly of "For The People" over the United Broadcasting Network) sched-uled to be heard online soon. URL: http://www.talkamerica.com/. E-mail: staff@talkamerica.com.

RA44 **Taylor Subscription Talk** *TST Audio-on-Demand.* A huge range of on-demand audio offerings, including a link to the outstanding **Radio Reading Services** (see above), with which it is affiliated. However, while some of this is free, much is available only for a fee. URL: http://www.tstradio.com/. E-mail: tstinfo@tstradio.com. Toll-free phone (U.S. only) (800) 789-4506.

RA44 **TBN** *Trinity Broadcasting Network.* Christian sermons and music, affiliated with CIRnet (see). Widely distributed programming. URL: http://www.tbn.org/audio.htm or http://cirnet.com/stations/tbn.htm. E-mail: (general) tbntalk@tbn.org, tbn@cirnet.com or chiser@tbn.org; (Webmaster) bmiller@tbn.org.

RA44 United Broadcasting Network. Various talk shows, often populist, including Bay Buchanan's ⊠ "For the People." URL: http://www.audionet.com/radio/talk/ubn/. E-mail: ubn@audionet.com. Toll-free phone (U.S. only) (800) 825-5937.

RA44 Vietnam Radio News Center Dài Phát Thanh Việt Nam. On-demand news in Vietnamese, covering international, national and California issues, as well as financial and other reports. URL: http://www.vietnamradio.com or http://206.86.148.162/leftframe/news/audionews.htm.

⊠ **RA44 VOA Voice of America.** Freshly on-demand audio, streamed and via file download, in English and other languages, from the official international broadcasting organization of the United States government. URL: (official VOA site, all languages) http://www.voa.gov/programs/audio/realaudio or http://www.wrn.org/stations/voa.html; (unofficial site, airing on-demand VOA news in Persian, Arabic, Hindi and Urdu only, plus Persian musical selections) http://gpg.com/radio/index.html. E-mail: (VOA) ke@voa.gov; (unofficial site) info@gpg.com.

RA44 Winston Cup Today NASCAR. On-demand interviews, news and commentary about NASCAR racing. Dozens of weekly half-hour and daily five-minute shows are archived, going back, like gestation, some nine months. URL: http://www.raceshop.com/wct/. E-mail: http://www.raceshop.com/comments.html.

United Nations

World Time –5 (–4 midyear) for New York Headquarters

⊠ **RA44 UNESCO Radio.** On-demand reports in English, French and Spanish. URL: http://www.nexus.org/Internet_Radio/ra-audio/MEMBERS/UNESCO/. E-mail: audio-visual@un.org.

⊠ **RA44 United Nations Environment and Population UNEP/PRB.** On-demand Global 500 reports in English concerning the UN Environment Program and the Population Reference Bureau. URL: http://www.nexus.org/Internet_Radio/ra-audio/UNEP/. E-mail: audio-visual@un.org.

⊠ **RA44 United Nations Radio.** On-demand World in Review and Scope and other programs in English and French. URL: (English and French, all programs, streamed) http://www.nexus.org/Internet_Radio/ra-audio/MEMBERS/UN_RADIO/; (English, World in Review and Scope only, streamed and via file download) http://www.wrn.org/stations/un.html. E-mail: audio-visual@un.org.

Prepared by the staff of PASSPORT TO WEB RADIO.

KUSF is one of the most creative stations on the Web.

CFRB•AM•1010 News Talk Radio   NEWS AND INFORMATION

Taylor Parnaby

Dave Agar

Mike Inglis

Donna Tranquada

Arnis Peterson

Mike Cleaver

Sheila Walsh

Guy Valentine

Monica Desantis

Voices from Canada

By-Province Guide to Web Radio Broadcasts

*T*ravelers and sports fans, Canadians have had access to all manner of traditional technologies to keep them abreast of the latest news, sports and information. Yet, until now most Canadian media choices have been out of reach.

Web radio has turned this on its head. There are already a score of Canadian selections—national as well as from eight cities in five provinces. Wherever in the world there's an Internet connection, now there's Canadian radio around the clock in English, French and other tongues. Many provide first-class listening even if you've never been in the country.

Canada

World Time –3:30 (–2:30 midyear) Newfoundland; –4 (–3 midyear) Atlantic; –5 (–4 midyear) Eastern, including Quebec and Ontario; –6 (–5 midyear) Central; except Saskatchewan; –6 Saskatchewan; –7 (–6 midyear) Mountain; –8 (–7 midyear) Pacific, including Yukon

Using three complementary technologies, Toronto's CFRB transmits locally over AM, regionally over world band radio and worldwide over Web radio. CFRB-CFRX

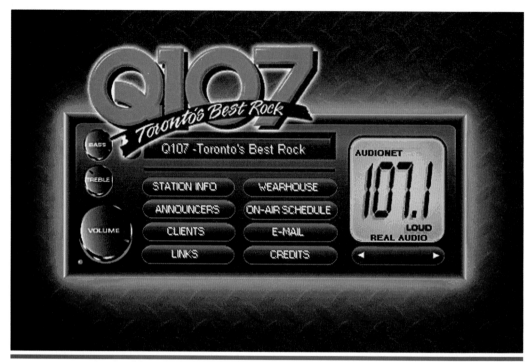

Rock, blues and interviews with musicians are the *menu du jour* every day of the week if you click onto Toronto's CILQ.

LOCAL

Alberta

Calgary

RA288 mono **CKUA 93.7 FM (if reactivated).** Formerly on RealAudio via Cadvision, CKUA hopes to reactivate this service in early 1997 as part of a provincially funded joint exercise with Athabasca University. A wide variety of music, from jazz to folk to blues to classic rock. Also, radio theater and news of the arts and other goings-on in Alberta. Programs are networked throughout Alberta on a variety of FM transmitters and one AM facility. URL: http://www.cadvision.com/ckua/. E-mail: ckua@oanet.com. Toll-free phone (Canada only): (800) 494-2582.

British Columbia

Vancouver

RA44 **CHMB AM 1320.** Live Chinese-language ethnic programming, plus a few archived song clips. URL: http://www.am1320.com/live/index.htm. E-mail: chmb@am1320.com or http://www.am1320.com/comments.html.

RA44 **CKNW/98 (if reactivated).** CKNW hopes to reactivate its

RealAudio service in an economic environment which is more munificent than that prevailing during its mid-1996 tests. Sports, news, talk, vintage radio, computer information, weather and self-help. URL: http://www.cknw.com/. E-mail: (general) info@cknw.com; (Webmaster) bob@cknw.com.

Newfoundland
Provincial

RA44 **NTV.** On-demand TV audio from the daily NTV Evening News Hour. NTV is viewed throughout the province over a number of VHF transmitters and via satellite. URL: http://www.newcomm.net/ftp/ntvnews/recent.ram. E-mail: (station) ntvnews@ntv.newcomm.net; (Webmaster) bdobbin@nlnet.nf.ca.

Local
St. John's

RA288 stereo **CHOZ OZ 94.7 FM.** Rock and weather in RealAudio 3.0 stereo. This sounds as good as any other station on the Web as of when we went to press, albeit with some echo and "stuttering" reminiscent of Max Headroom—both characteristic of beta v3.0 on 28.8 connections (ISDN links fare much better). URL: http://www.ozfm.newcomm.net/. E-mail:

(general) ozfm@newcomm.net; (webmaster) bdobbin@nlnet.nf.ca.
RA288 mono **VOCM 590 AM.** Live coverage of the St. John's Maple Leafs AHL hockey games, with commentary by Brian Rogers and Tom Ormsby, but otherwise no regular programming over the Web. URL: http://www.newcomm.net/sjleafs/live/default.htm. E-mail: sjleafs@newcomm.net or http://www.newcomm.net/sjleafs/guest/guest.htm.

Ontario

Brampton

RA288 stereo **RA288** mono **CIAO 530 AM Polskie Radio Toronto.** Live ethnic Polish news, talk and music. URL: http://ituner.com/530AM/. E-mail: (station) zeranski@io.org; (Webmaster) prt@ituner.com.

Ottawa

StreamWorks 2.0 **CFRA 580.** News, talk and sports, including live coverage of the Montréal Expos, Ottawa Rough Riders, Ottawa Senators and Toronto Raptors. URL: http://www.cfra.com/ or http://www.3wb.com/listen.html. E-mail: mailbox@koolcfra.com or http://www.planetkool.com/info.htm#email. Toll-free phone (North America only): (800) 580-2372.

CHMB serves Vancouver's large ethnic Chinese community, including many formerly from Hong Kong, on 1320 kHz AM. Starting in 1996, it has also been reaching a worldwide audience over Web radio.

CILQ

After a year's absence, the popular Jesse & Gene morning show is back on the air at Q107 in Toronto. "We're a pain in the gas," quips a smiling Gene Valaitis.

StreamWorks 2.0 (56+ kb modems only) **CKKL KOOL 93.9.** Rock, including Sunday's World Chart Show with top hits from around the world...but only if you're wired at high-speed ISDN or better. URL: http://www.3wb.com/listen.html. E-mail: (general) mailbox@koolcfra.com or jay@planetkool.com; (World Chart Show) worldchart@aol.com; (staffers) http://www.planetkool.com/info.htm#email.

Scarborough

RA288 mono **CHIR-FM Greek Radio Station.** News and soccer from Greece, Greek ethnic news, plus Greek entertainment and delightful Greek music—all presented in Greek. As of press time, audio quality and reliability were not what they should be, but their Webmaster is interested in knowing if these problems continue. URL: http://www.chir.com/noframe.htm. E-mail: (station) comments@chir.com; (Webmaster) webmaster@dapa.com. Toll-free phone: (Canada and U.S. only) (888) 467-2447.

Toronto (also see Brampton)

RA288 mono **CFNY 102.1 the EDGE.** Expects to air live over Web Radio in the very near future. New rock, plus news and sports reports. URL: http://edge.passport.ca/. E-mail: earl2@passport.ca, edge@passport.ca or x@passport.ca.

RA44 **CFRB-CFRX AM 1010.** News, weather, talk and garden shows are live and, for some programs, also on-demand, including "The Best of CFRB." Although this site bills itself as unauthorized, it is well-laid-out and handy. URL: http://www.io.org/~iain/CFRB/. E-mail: iain@io.org.

StreamWorks 2.0 **CFTR 680News.** All news, either live via StreamWorks or downloaded news headlines in .wav files. URL: http://www.canoe.ca/680News/.

RA288 mono **CHOG Talk 640.** News and talk. URL: http://www.talk640.com/taudio.htm. E-mail: (news) talk640news@talk640.wic.ca; (webmaster) dhuzar@inforamp.net.

RA44 **CHUM 1050 The Oldies Station.** Cry your hearts old, early Boomers and duck-tailed Fiftysomethings, because this Grade-A oldies station offers *nary a minute of live audio!* And, they tell us, they don't plan to anytime soon. Instead, you can check out a smattering nostalgic on-demand interviews with some of the leading lights of Fifties and Sixties rock 'n' roll (okay, with some Seventies types thrown in for good measure). With the genuine oldies format having all but disappeared from the airwaves, this station is exactly the type that should be streaming and screaming over Web radio, preferably in RealAudio 3.0. *Que será será.* URL: http://www.1050chum.com/index.html. E-mail: webmaster@ 1050chum.com; (requests) http://www.1050chum.com/ 1050-2/1050-2.html. RA288 mono **CILQ Q107.** Rock, plus an hour of blues Sunday night.

URL: (RealAudio; a new or replacement audio URL may activate shortly) http://www.q107.com/qaudio.html; (text) http://www.q107.com/ hiq107.html. E-mail: (webmaster) dhuszar@q107.wic.ca; (music staff) qmusic@inforamp.net. Toll-free phone (Canada only): (800) 668-7625.

Quebec

Montréal

RA44 **CBC/CBF 690 AM.** News and features in French from Canada's leading French-language public radio station. URL: (if you get a rejection error, keep trying) http:// www.radio-canada.com/ radiodirect/index.html. E-mail: auditoire@ montreal.src.ca.

"3WB" is the Web umbrella site for Ottawa's CKKL-FM and sister station CFRA-AM. CFRA airs live coverage of the Montréal Expos, Ottawa Rough Riders, Ottawa Senators and Toronto Raptors. Also, news, talk and sports reports.

NATIONAL AND INTERNATIONAL

RA288 stereo and mono **RA44** **CBC** A wide range of CBC domestic and international radio offerings from this Web site for the entire CBC. URL: http://www.cbc.ca/index.html. E-mail: (program feedback) cbcinput@toronto.cbc.ca; (webmaster) info@radio.cbc.ca; (hyperlink to other e-mail addresses) http://www.cbc.ca/aboutcbc/address/address.html.

RA44 **CBC Chaîne Radio FM.** Cultural programming, including music, drama, documentaries and discussions, produced in Montréal in French. URL: (if you get a rejection error, keep trying) http://www.radio-canada.com/radiodirect/index.html. E-mail: auditoire@montreal.src.ca.

RA288 stereo and mono **CBC Stereo.** URL: (live in stereo) http://www.cbc.ca/ or

CFNY

Pete Fowler, whose interests include levitation and baking, can be heard at various times on Toronto's CFNY, 102.1 the EDGE.

http://radioworks.cbc.ca; (RealTime on-demand and live concerts in stereo and mono) http://www.cbcstereo.com/RealTime/soundz/realaudio/index.html or http://realtime.cbcstereo.com. E-mail: (RealTime) realtime@cbcstereo.com; (other) see **CBC**, above.

RA288 mono Internet Wave **ITV News**, Edmonton. On-demand TV audio from this Alberta-based TV network with TV affiliates in Red Deer, Lethbridge, Victoria, Calgary and Hamilton, and a radio affiliate in Toronto. URL: (RealAudio) http://www.itv.ca/RAtest.htm or http://www.itv.ca/whatsnew.htm; (Internet Wave) http://www.itv.ca/sotw.htm. E-mail: http://www.itv.ca/email.htm.

RA44 **Radio Canada International**, Montreal. Ten minutes of on-demand news in English, French, Arabic, Chinese, Russian, Spanish and Ukrainian; also, live feed of whatever language and program happens to be going out over world band radio at the time. URL: (on-demand RealAudio news in English and other languages, plus text) http://www.rcinet.ca/en/actual/news/news.htm; (on-demand RealAudio news, streamed and file download, in English) http://www.wrn.org/stations/rci.html; (live RealAudio feed in various languages) http://www.rcinet.ca/en/index.htm; ("Quirks and Quarks" RealAudio and .au on-demand

For some real Northern Exposure, click onto Ottawa's CKKL, KOOL FM. CKKL's rock format is supplemented Sundays by the World Chart Show, playing top hits from around the world. But unlike virtually every other Web radio station, CKKL requires that you have an ISDN connection.

science program in English) http://www.radio.cbc.ca/radio/programs/current/quirks/archives.htm; (limited text) http://radioworks.cbc.ca/radio/rci/rci.html. E-mail: rci@montreal.src.ca or http://www.rcinet.ca/en/infos/courr.htm.

DISESTABLISHMENTARIAN

⌧ (RA₄₄) **"Voice of Freedom" ("Stimme der Freiheit")**, Toronto. Once prosecuted in Canada for his Holocaust-denial stance, Ernst Zündel and his Web "Zündelsite"are

among the chief reasons Germany and other governments want laws drawn up to keep rightist propaganda off the Internet. However odious this site's attempts to turn facts upside down, for some it may be worth visiting to get a sense of the debate over freedom of speech on the Internet. URL: http://www.webcom.com/~ezundel/english/aaa.address.html. E-mail: ezundel@cts.com.

_____

Prepared by the staff of PASSPORT TO WEB RADIO.

Latin American Sounds

¡Hola, Amigos y Compatriotas!

From Colombia's Onda Caliente to the rhythms of Brazil, Latin America offers some of the most interesting listening over the air, and now on the Web. Although Latin American Web radio is very much in its infancy, it's likely to be among the fastest-growing in the years to come.

Argentina

World Time –3 Buenos Aires and eastern provinces; –4 in some western provinces.

LOCAL

Buenos Aires

RA288 stereo **RA288** mono **Emisiones Platenses FM 92.1 Cada Día Más.** Live rock, hip-hop and pop hits, mostly in English and Spanish, from the Sixties, Seventies and Eighties—all presented in mono in Spanish over this

Venus Radio rocks Asunción live over FM and on-demand over Web radio. Venus Radio

Brazil's Iguaçu Falls, on the border with Argentina and near a region of Paraguay where contraband is widespread, is considered to be the Eighth Wonder of The World. Also nearby, on the Paraná River, is the world's largest hydroelectric complex.

award-winning station. Individual hits can also be heard on-demand, jukebox style, in mono or stereo. Page downloads can be painfully slow, so go directly to the page with the programming you want. URL: (live, plus introductory clips—click on Escúchanos EN VIVO!!) http://www.hoy.netverk.com.ar/la92/; (on-demand menu of Top 40 hits) http://www.hoy.netverk.com.ar/la92/RankingSemana.html; (on-demand menu of #1 hits of the last four weeks) http://www.hoy.netverk.com.ar/la92/ClasicoSemana.html; (if preceding URLs fail) http://www.h-span.net/livrasp.htm. E-mail: fm92@netverk.com.ar or http://

www.hoy.netverk.com.ar/la92/addguest.html.

RA44 Radio Mitre AM 80 LR6. On-demand half-hour *último noticiero* in Spanish from one of Argentina's premier news sources. URL: http://www.clarin.com/index.html. E-mail: soporte@www.clarin.com.

Córdoba

RA44 Radio Córdoba AM 70 LV3. On-demand newscast, updated every 12 hours, and sports summary in Spanish. URL: http://200.26.95.98/cor/sintesis.htm; or http://www.lv3.com.ar/cor. E-mail: (station) lv3@lv3.com.ar; (Webmaster) brizuela@sucesos.com.

Brazil

World Time −1 (−2 midyear) Atlantic Islands; −2 (−3 midyear) Eastern, including Brasília and Rio de Janeiro, plus the town of Barra do Garças; −3 (−4 midyear) Western; −4 (−5 midyear) Acre. Some northern states keep midyear time year round.

☞ PCs are a big thing in Brazil, so look for more activity. To keep current, check the hyperlink http://www.usp.br/geral/cultura/emissora.html. For now, bandwidth in Brazil is not all it could be, so expect connection problems and brief pauses during re-buffering. If no luck with the first try, come back later, as servers tend to be down or occupied more often than usual.

Belo Horizonte

Rádio Itatiaia 610/5970 kHz A Rádio de Minas (when operating). Brazilian popular music, news, live soccer and sports commentary presented in Portuguese. URL: (click on RealAudio icon) http://www.itatiaia.com.br/som/index.html. E-mail: itatiaia@ itatiaia.com.br.
Rádio 98 FM. Current and classic rock, presented live in Portuguese when their RealAudio server is operating. URL: http://www.98fm.com.br/98real.htm or http://www.bhnet.com.br/98fm/98real.htm. E-mail: radio@98fm.com.br.

Recife

Rádio Jornal UFPE (if activated). Station of the Universidade Federal de Pernambuco, with pro-

Fans of Brazilian soccer will want to tune in to Rádio Itatiaia, which reaches abroad on both Web radio and world band radio.

Holding de Radio

Humberto Rubín founded Radio Ñandutí in 1962. Because of Rubín's opposition to the Stroessner regime, the station was jammed, as well as closed down on several occasions. Now the regime is history, and Ñandutí is heard worldwide.

grams in Portuguese. However, the site is under construction, with Web radio thus far only a hope. URL: http://www.di.ufpe.br or http://www.radio-jornal.di.ufpe.br. E-mail: (general) jftm@di.ufpe.br; (Webmaster) webmaster@di.ufpe.br.

São Paulo

RA28.8 mono **RA44** Shockwave 28.8 **A Rádio Rock 89.1 FM.** Currently testing on-demand rock songs and station clips, mainly in RealAudio but partly in Shockwave,

with live audio in Portuguese possibly in the offing. URL: (general audio and text offerings) http://www.rockwave.com/89/; (clip of normal programming) http://www.rockwave.com/89/ra.htm. E-mail: guilherme@rockwave.com or http://www.rockwave.com/89/interact.htm.
RA44 **Clube 100,5 FM.** Top-40 hits, presented in Portuguese, when the connection is successful. URL: (click on Clique aqui... atop the page) http://www.convex.com.br/clube/clubefm.html. E-mail: clubefm@convex.com.br.

Colombia

World Time –5

☞ To check on the latest additions to the Caracol network of stations on Web radio, go to the hyperlink http://latina.latino.net.co/empresa/caracol/caracol.htm.

NATIONAL

RA44 **Radioactiva Nacional 88.5 (Caracol)**, Santafé de Bogotá. Latino pop and rock, news and live soccer, all presented live in Spanish from this station heard throughout Colombia on 16 FM transmitters. Also, Top-40 hits and other clips on-demand. On-demand audio works well, but live feed can be frustratingly balky. Station is considering upgrading to

28.8 kb before long. URL: (live) http://
www.radioactiva.com/; (Top-40 "jukebox" of Spanish songs) http://
www.radioactiva.com/programa/
top40/top40.html; (TV audio clip)
http://www.radioactiva.com/programa/
laloco/momentos.html; (if other URLs
fail) http://www.h-span.net/
OTRARASP.htm. E-mail: (general)
radioactiva@olga.latino.net.co;
(guest book) http://olga.latino.net.co/
performpro/pro_gstbook/submit.htm;
(Caracol) latino@sin.com.co.

NATIONAL/INTERNATIONAL

Tropical Latino (Caracol).
Popular Latino rhythms from this first-
rate hour-and-a-half Caracol show
that's aired each Saturday over some
80 radio stations throughout Latin
America, plus Spain and France. The
last two weeks' shows are available
on demand in RealAudio 14.4, but
they are seriously considering moving
to 28.8 before long. *¡Escuche!* URL:
http://tropical.latino.net.co/
esta_semana/Index.htm. E-mail: (program) tropical@olga.latino.net.co;
(Caracol) latino@sin.com.co.

Honduras

World Time –6

**HRJA *Radio Copán
Internacional.*** For now, only a couple
of quarter-hour English-language on-
demand features on Honduras are
being carried on Web radio. URL:
http://www.nexus.org/Internet_Radio/
ra-audio/OTHER/. E-mail:
71163.1735@compuserve.com.

Although it's not the easiest to hear, Radio El Espectador offers a wide variety of on-demand
news, sports and features—*todo en español.*

 El Partido en **12"**

Montevideo's Radio Oriental offers top-notch soccer games live from Uruguay's capital.

Mexico

World Time –6 (–5 midyear) Central, including D.F.; –7 (–6 midyear) Mountain; –8 (–7 midyear) Pacific

LOCAL

Mexico City

XHB Radioactivo 98.5. Hispanic and other rock, presented live and in Spanish, although the RealAudio player is occasionally inoperative. In order to use this site, you have to first give your assigned alias and password. Among other questions they ask when you apply for these is your age, but the upper limit allowed is 50, so be prepared to fib if you're in your second half-century. URL: (audio) http://www.radioactivo.com.mx/98.5/transmision.html; (to get alias and password the first time you listen) http://www.radioactivo.com.mx/encuesta.html?Nuevo+Usuario=Nuevo+Usuario; (if preceding URLs fail) http://www.h-span.net/livrasp.htm. E-mail: ricardo@radioactivo.com.mx,

aflores@radioactivo.com.mx,
hinclan@radioactivo.com.mx or
wilson@radioactivo.com.mx.

NATIONAL/INTERNATIONAL

RA44 Informe de Gobierno. A variety
of official on-demand news communi-
ques in Spanish. URL: http://
www.infosel.com.mx/extra/informe/
informe.htm or http://www.h-span.net/
OTRARASP.htm. E-mail:
jesus@visatel.net.

RA44 K-INT, Mexico City. On-demand
news and analysis, as well as financial reports and various features
about Mexico, all in Spanish from this
Internet-only station. Nominally operates at 28.8 kb, but in reality it's 14.4
kb—usually streamed, but sometimes
via file download. URL: http://
www.mpsnet.com.mx/k-int/. E-mail:
(general) kint@mpsnet.com.mx or
http://www.mpsnet.com.mx/k-int/
kintreg.html; (Webmaster)
katyna@mpsnet.com.mx.

R. Sarandí

Radio Sarandí presents freshly updated on-
demand news and features from its state-of-
the-art offices in Montevideo, Uruguay.

counter, near end of long page)
siglonet@pananet.com.

Paraguay

World Time –3 (–4 midyear)

☞ All Paraguayan stations, below,
operate RealAudio via Infonet. Sometimes its RealAudio service is on,
sometimes it's off.

Asunción

RA288 mono **Radio Ñandutí AM ZP14 La
Gran Emisora Paraguaya.** News,
business news, commentary and related features in Spanish from the
flagship station of the Rubín family
("Holding de Radio"). URL: http://
www.infonet.com.py/holding/
nanduam/nanduam.htm; also, check

Panama

LOCAL/NATIONAL

Panamá City

**RA44 K.W. Continente Radio Reloj
Continente 700.** On-demand half-
hour news in Spanish. URL: http://
www.elsiglo.com/. E-mail: (icon above

Deejay Clari Arias with "Venus Girls" Victoria, Carolina and Irma during the presentation of the Venus *Dance Hits* CD in July, 1996.

at possible new ISP's site of http://www.quanta.com.py. E-mail: holding@infonet.com.py.

Venus 105.1 *Tu Radio.* On-demand Top Ten rock hits, mostly Latin American, but no live feed as yet. URL: http://www.infonet.com.py/venus/topten/index.htm. E-mail: venus@infonet.com.py.

Pedro Juan Caballero

Radio Mburucuyá AM 980 kHz. News and courageous commentary in Spanish and Guaraní, including from Radio Cadena Nacional, with emphasis on affairs in the Departamento de Amambay along the Brazilian border. The Web site shows Santiago Leguizamón, the station's original owner, who was gunned down in an ambush a few years back because the station refused to tone down its fight against narco-corruption and gangland violence that was, and is, widespread in the area. URL: http://www.infonet.com.py/holding/mburu/mburu.htm. E-mail: holding@infonet.com.py.

San Bernardino

RA44 **Rock & Pop 95.5 FM.** Just what it says, this Rubín family operation airs a mix of Latin American and English-language songs hosted in Spanish. URL: http://www.infonet.com.py/holding/rock/rock.htm. E-mail: holding@infonet.com.py.

Uruguay

World Time –3

Montevideo

RA44 **Radio El Espectador.** On-demand news, sports and other material in Spanish, but requires time-consuming file downloading, as there is no streamed audio. URL: http://www.zfm.com/espectador/. E-mail: espectad@zfm.com.

RA288 mono **Radio Oriental CX12.** On-demand and live material, including soccer games, in Spanish. URL: http://netgate.comintur.com.uy/cx12/. E-mail: cx12@netgate.comintur.com.uy.

RA44 **Radio Sarandí AM 690.** The *en vivo* Web page heading notwithstanding, all Sarandí's many Spanish-language news and other offerings are on-demand. However, they are freshly updated, the audio is streamed—not downloaded—and even at 14.4 kb the audio quality is crisp and superior. URL: (RealAudio) http://netgate.comintur.com.uy/sarandi/envivo.html; (text) http://lsa.lsa.com.uy/sarandi. E-mail: sarandi@lsa.lsa.com.uy.

Prepared by the staff of Passport to Web Radio.

Mexico's on the Web! Not only is there live FM from Mexico City, there are also two stations heard only on Web radio, K-INT carries the latest news and analysis, along with other features and financial reports.

European Radio Online

Passport to Web Radio from Ireland to Russia

Whether it's midnight in Moscow or lunch in Lugano, the sounds of Europe are but a mouse-click away. Some are in English, others in native tongues—an Old World bouillabaisse, with fresh perspectives on the news and leading-edge entertainment.

Austria

World Time +1 (+2 midyear)

LOCAL

Linz

RA44 Österreichischer Rundfunk Radio Oberösterreich 95.2 FM. On-demand international, national and local news, as well as live stock-exchange activity, in German. URL: http://radio-o.orf.at/demand.htm. E-mail: koenigs@ibm.net.

NATIONAL

RA44 Österreichischer Rundfunk Blue Danube Radio. On-demand news in English and German from the ORF's BDR domestic network. URL: (RealAudio, streamed, and file

Nothing beats a stay in Paris, but now you can tune in everything from France Info to the Sorbonne on Web radio. Digital Stock

111

Yes, Virginia, there really is a Radio Mafia—Radiomafia, actually. But it's in Finland, not Sicily, and is scheduled to start airing over Web radio by the end of May. They give out free bumper stickers, too, if you want to keep fellow motorists from tailgating.

download) http://www.wrn.org/stations/danube.html; (text, ORF) http://www.orf.at/teletext/570.htm; (text and .wav audio clips, Friends of Blue Danube Radio) http://www.via.at/fobdr/main.htm. E-mail: (general) bdr-tas@orf.at or fm4@orf.at; (Friends of Blue Danube Radio) 100071.1652@compuserve.com.

INTERNATIONAL

🗙 **RAI44** **Radio Austria International.** "Report from Austria" newscast in English and German on demand from the official international broadcaster for Austria. URL: (RealAudio, streamed, and file download) http://www.wrn.org/stations/orf.html; (text) http://www.orf.at/rai/uk/uk_home.htm. E-mail: info@rai.ping.at.

Belgium

World Time +1 (+2 midyear)

🗙 **RAI44** **Radio Vlaanderen Internationaal.** Programs in English and Dutch on demand from the official international broadcaster for

Belgium's Flemish community. URL: (RealAudio, streamed, and file download) http://www.wrn.org/stations/rvi.html; (ditto, plus text) http://www.brtn.be/rvi/html-uk/waar/index.htm. E-mail: rvi@brtn.be.

Croatia

World Time +1 (+2 midyear)

⚏ **RA44** **Croatian Radio.** On-demand and live news and features in Croatian, with brief newscasts in English. URL: http://www.matis.hr/radio/, http://vukovar.unm.edu/hic/radio/ or http://hic.hrvati.aus.net/radio/. E-mail: radio@matis.hr, http://www.tel.hr/matis/radio/survey.html, http://vukovar.unm.edu/hic/radio/survey.html or http://hic.hrvati.aus.net/radio/survey.html.

Czech Republic

World Time +1 (+2 midyear)

LOCAL

Brno
RA288 mono **Radio Kiss Hády 88.3 FM.** Current rock, mostly non-Czech, along with some news—all presented in Czech. URL: (RealAudio) http://www.cz./cgi-bin/cz?asc=/ra/ default.html; (text and RealAudio) http://www.cz./kiss/. E-mail: (station) kisshady@brno.bohem-net.cz; (Webmaster) www@www.cz.

INTERNATIONAL

⚏ **RA44** **Radio Prague.** On-demand news and interesting features, including nose-recognition contests, in RealAudio and via file download. URL: (direct) http://www.radio.cz; (via U.K.) http://www.wrn.org/stations/prague.html; (via Canada) http://www.ituner.com/ee.htm. E-mail: (general) cr@radio.cz; (Czech Department) palka@radio.cz; (English Department) english@radio.cz; (Canadian site) ee-radio@ituner.com.

INTERNATIONAL (OTHER)

⚏ mono **RA44** **RFE-RL.** First experimented with RealAudio when Hillary Clinton visited Prague in 1996. This station, which resulted from the merger of the former Radio Free Europe and Radio Liberty stations, airs on-demand news and features in a wide variety of Eastern European and Russian-related languages. URL: http://www.rferl.org/realaudio/index.html. E-mail: (administration) klose@rferl.org; (Webmaster) websitemanager@rferl.org.

A good station to Czech out is Radio Kiss Hády, 88.3 FM in Brno in the former Czechoslovakia. It's live and in Czech, and carries lots of music.

Denmark

World Time +1 (+2 midyear)

⌘ **Danmarks Radio.** Half an hour of on-demand noon-edition news in Danish from the domestic network. Alas, the English program aired occasionally via DR's "Radio Danmark" has been dropped for now, but comments concerning reviving it are welcomed. URL: http://www.dr.dk/. E-mail: rdk@dr.dk or webmaster@dr.dk.

Finland

World Time +2 (+3 midyear)

☞ For a country of only five million people with a language rarely understood outside its borders, Finland is nicely represented over Web radio. For now, a number of YLE stations only offer audio clips, but this could evolve into streamed RealAudio in due course. All stations accept correspondence in English, Finnish and Swedish.

LOCAL

Helsinki

StreamWorks 2.0 **KissFM *102.4.*** Rock music, presented in Finnish, plus "DATE," a correspondence window for young men wishing to get acquainted with young ladies, or the other way round. (Don't know Finnish? Most young Finns are proficient in English!) URL: (general, including RealAudio) http://www.kiss.fi/ (click "Radio On"); ("DATE," when it is actually functioning) http://www.kiss.fi/date.shtml. E-mail: (general) wwwadmin@kiss.fi; ("DATE") ulla@kiss.fi.

Oulu

.wav **YLE/Radio Suomi OULU 97.3.** All that's available at this marginal site are some file downloads of audio clips in Finnish. URL: http://www.yle.fi/ radiosuomi/oulu/index.html. E-mail: http://www.yle.fi/radiosuomi/oulu/ toimitus.html.

Pori

RA144 YLE/Satakunnan Radio 94.8. Two brief audio clips in Finnish are the slim pickings from this local pop station. URL: http://www.yle.fi/ sataradio/front.html. E-mail (indirectly): virjaka@cc.spt.fi.

Tampere

StreamWorks 2.0 **Radio Moro.** Rock, old and new—live as well as on-demand musical cuts—all presented in Finnish on FM for Tampere and well beyond. URL: http://www.alexpress.fi/moro/. E-mail: http://www.alexpress.fi/moro/ palaute.html.

NATIONAL

RA288 mono **YLE-2 Radiomafia (when activated).** Before the end of May, 1997, this popular Finnish-language station is to go onto Web radio with its usual mix of rock, jazz and ethnic music, as well as news of musical and other cultural happenings. URL: http://www.yle.fi/radiomafia/ English.html. E-mail: jorma.jortikka@yle.fi.

.au **YLE/Radio Suomi.** Various brief items in Finnish, on-demand via patience-trying file download, plus a link to the much-more-satisfactory YLE/Radio Uutiset in RealAudio (see below to go direct). URL: http:// www.yle.fi/radiosuomi/. E-mail: radiosuomi@radiosuomi.yle.fi.

RA144 YLE/Radio Uutiset. The latest on-demand news headlines in Finnish from Radio Suomi's YLE/Radionews. URL: http://www.yle.fi/radiouutiset/ uutiset.htm. E-mail: (general) radiouutiset@yle.fi; (specific staffers) http://www.yle.fi/radiouutiset/ toimitus.htm.

RA288 mono **YLE/Radio X (if activated).** Rock and alternative rock presented in Swedish on FM throughout parts of Finland and audible in parts of Sweden, and they hope to add RealAudio to extend their reach. URL: http:// www.yle.fi/radiox/Info/ index.shtml#english. E-mail: leena.viitala@yle.fi.

INTERNATIONAL AND NATIONAL

RA144 Ear Mountain Radio The Official Santa Claus Radio Station, North Pole. Decembers only, Santa Claus fires up his little radio station, Joulupukki Radioasema, for all the boys and girls of the world to hear . . . provided they have access to a PC and modem. URL: http://www.nettiradio.fi/test/santa/saneng.htm. E-mail: nettir@tomin.pp.fi. ⊞ **(RA44) YLE/Radio Finland.** Live and on-demand news and features for foreign audiences and expatriate and traveling Finns in English, Finnish, French, German, Russian and Swedish. On-demand audio is available on both RealAudio and file download. URL: http://www.yle.fi/fbc/radiofin.html or http://www.wrn.org/stations/yle.html. E-mail: rfinland@yle.mailnet.fi or yleus@aol.com.

France

World Time +1

LOCAL/REGIONAL

Gironde (Bordeaux-Médoc)

(RA288) mono Europe 2 Le Meilleur de la Musique, Bordeaux. This national rock and hip-hop network isn't audible live via its headquarters in Paris, but never fear—it's loud and clear from its Sud Ouest regional offices in Bordeaux. URL: http://www.europe2.altantel.fr/. E-mail: (station) europe2@atlantel.fr; (Webmaster) atlantel@atlantel.fr.

(RA288) mono Skyrock 102.8, Bordeaux. Rock music, presented in French. URL: (click en direct) http://www.skyrock.atlantel.fr/. E-mail: (station) skyrock@atlantel.fr; (Webmaster) atlantel@atlantel.fr.

StreamWorks 2.0 Wit-FM, Bordeaux. Rock and pop, much of it French, presented in French, along with interspersed bits of telephone banter. URL: (click on the lower cliquez ici) http://www.quaternet.fr:8081/live/ecoute1.html. E-mail: (general) live@quaternet.fr; (Webmaster) webmaster@quaternet.fr.

NATIONAL

StreamWorks 2.0 Europe 1. On-demand news updated six times a day, plus weather, sports results and a financial report in French, with more items to be offered in the future. Unfortunately, all programs are time-delayed by an hour before they are made available on the Web. URL: (audio menu is near top of page) http://www.francelink.com/radio_stations/europe1/europe1.html. E-mail: (Webmaster) webmaster@francelink.com.

(RA44) Europe 2. For now, only audio clips of popular music and such in RealAudio and via file download from Europe 2's Paris headquarters. However, Europe 2 is audible live via its Bordeaux outlet (see above). URL: http://www.europe2.fr/radioclip/index.html. E-mail: anim_e2@europe2.fr.

(RA44) France Info. Fresh and other news on-demand in French. URL: http://www.radio-france.fr/. E-mail: http://www.radio-france.fr/general/message.htm.

RA288 mono **France 3.** TV audio, with on-demand news in French. URL: http://www.sv.vtcom.fr/ftv/fr3/infos/infos.html. E-mail: tvte13@france3.fr.

RA288 mono **Fun Radio.** Rock and hip-hop, live and in French from this private network with FM outlets throughout the Hexagon. URL: http://www.funradio.fr/funlive/home-funlive.html. E-mail: florian@funradio.fr.

StreamWorks 2.0 **RTL.** On-demand news updated six times a day, plus weather, sports reports and horoscope in French, with more items to be offered in the future. Unfortunately, all programs are time-delayed by an hour before they are made available on the Web. URL: (audio menu is near top of page) http://www.francelink.com/radio_stations/rtl/rtl.html. E-mail: (station, but it works best if you also send a copy of your message to the Webmaster) 101317.1102@compuserve.com; (Webmaster) webmaster@francelink.com.

RA288 mono **RTL 2.** Rock, live and in French, along with newscasts, from this popular network with FM outlets throughout France. URL: (click wherever it says "en direct". http://www.rtl2.fr/. E-mail: (general) schembri@rtl2.fr; (quiz) http://www.rtl2.fr/cgi-bin/jeu.cgi.

StreamWorks 2.0 **Sorbonne—Radio France.** Always wanted to attend the Sorbonne and hang out with literati in Left Bank cafés? Well, now's your chance to make up for at least the classroom part of what you've missed.

Sorbonne—Radio France offers lectures on a wide variety of subjects, and you won't even have to stand out in the hall to hear them. Being French courses, they're in French, of course. URL: http://www.francelink.com/radio_stations/sorbonne/srfgrille.html. E-mail: (Webmaster) webmaster@francelink.com.

☞ If this sort of activity interests you, also check out http://www.edufrance.org/.

INTERNATIONAL

StreamWorks 2.0 **France Fréquence.** Numerous on-demand features in French, plus musical selections, for French men and women in North America and elsewhere abroad. Prepared in Washington, where the French government has made a major commitment to the Internet for propagating French culture and information. URL: (audio menu is near top of page) http://www.francelink.com/radio_stations/ff/ff.html. E-mail: (Washington) gary.dwor@amb-wash.fr; (Webmaster) webmaster@francelink.com.

⊠ **RA44** **StreamWorks** 2.0 **Radio France Internationale.** On-demand news and features in English and French from France's official international broadcaster. URL: (**RA44** English and French news, streamed and via file download) http://www.wrn.org/stations/rfi.html; (**StreamWorks** 2.0 French news and

RTL 2 airs news and rocks France—and now, thanks to Web radio, the world. *Animateur radio* Alexis keeps listeners entertained while noshing his favorite goodie, Black Forest cake.

features, streamed) http://www.francelink.com/radio_stations/rfi/rfi.html. E-mail: fenyo@eunet.fr.

Germany

World Time +1 (+2 midyear)

REGIONAL

Bavaria

Streamworks 2.0 **Bayerischer Rundfunk-Bayern 5.** Live and on-demand news and other programming in German. URL: http://br.gmd.de/b5akt/b1.html.

E-mail: http://br.gmd.de/cgi-bin/feedback.

Eastern Germany-Berlin

RA44 **SFB/ORB** *InfoRadio.* Live regional, national and international news in German. URL: http://www.inforadio.de/. E-mail: kru@pr-kruithof.b.eunet.de.

Southern Germany-Stuttgart

RA44 **SDR 1 Radio.** On-demand newscast in German. URL: (click on ++Nachrichten++ or Hier gibt's was zu hören . . .) http://www.sdr.de/radio/sdr1/nachrichten/index.html. E-mail: info@sdr.de or http://www.sdr.de/feedback/index.html.

INTERNATIONAL

⊠ **RA44** **Deutsche Welle** *Voice of Germany.* On-demand audio in English, German, French, Portuguese, Russian, Spanish, Turkish and other languages from Germany's official international broadcaster. URL: (all languages except German) http://www-dw.gmd.de/DW/1.01/; (German radio) http://www-dw.gmd.de/DW/; (German TV-Nachrichten news audio, with English in the offing) http://www.dmc.net/dw/dw.html or http://www.mainnet.dmc.net/dw/dw.html; (English, streamed and via file download) http://www.wrn.org/stations/dw.html. E-mail: (general) dw@dw.gmd.de; (TV audio) dmc@dmc.net.

Greece

World Time +2 (+3 midyear)

LOCAL

Athens

RA288 mono **Radio Gold 105.** Oldies from the Fifties through the Seventies presented in Greek. URL: (click on station's "highway" logo) http://www.hol.gr/radiogold/. E-mail (English or Greek): webmaster@prometheus.hol.gr or http://www.hol.gr/cgi-bin/ Send?Webmaster.

Holland (The Netherlands)

World Time +1 (+2 midyear)

NATIONAL

RA288 mono .wav **Radio 3 FM Spoor 7**, Hilversum. On-demand streamed and downloaded clips of modern Christian music and other odd bits from this regular radio program. URL: http://www.omroep.nl/eo/spoor7/ra/ welcome.html. E-mail: spoor7@eo.nl.

INTERNATIONAL

RA44 **Radio Nederland Wereldomroep *Radio Netherlands.*** On-demand news and features in English and Dutch via streamed or file download from Holland's official international broadcasting station. URL: http://www.wrn.org/stations/ rnw.html. E-mail: letters@rnw.nl.

Hungary

World Time +1 (+2 midyear)

NATIONAL

RA44 **Magyar Rádió 1 *Kossuth Rádió.*** Music, mostly rock, plus news and features, mainly in Hungarian. URL: (click on any of the three "Szerver" icons) http:// www.kossuth.enet.hu/online.html. E-mail: e-net@enet.hu.

RA44 **Magyar Rádió 2 *Petőfi Rádió.*** First-rate traditional Hungarian music makes this station a treat for the ears. It also carries news and other items in Hungarian, but it's the music that'll bring you back again and again. URL: (click on any of the three "Szerver" icons) http:// www.petofi.enet.hu/reala.html. E-mail: petofi.radio@enet.hu.

INTERNATIONAL

RA44 **Radio Budapest.** On-demand news and features in English, German and Hungarian, via streaming and file download. URL: http://

www.wrn.org/stations/hungary.html.
E-mail: (English and Hungarian)
ango11@kaf.radio.hu; (German)
nemetl@kaf.radio.hu.

Iceland

World Time exactly

⊠ (RA44) **Ríkisútvarpid**, Reykjavík. On-demand 15-minute newscast (click on "Samantekt innlendra frétta"), along with brief audio clips, all in Icelandic from Iceland's national broadcaster. URL: http://this.is/ruv/. E-mail (English or Icelandic): thisisruv@ruv.is or heimirs@ruv.is.

Ireland (Eire)

World Time exactly (+1 midyear)

NATIONAL

(RA44) **Radio Telefís Eireann 2FM.**
National news, on-demand and streamed, plus streamed pop and Top-40 music, winning lottery numbers and convivial chat—all done with a thoroughly Irish flair. Also, live interviews with, and performances from, Irish musicians. Most programs originate from the main studios in Dublin, but some emanate from Cork, Limerick, Sligo and Waterford, plus a mobile studio that transmits from around

the country. URL: http://live.websters.ie/broadcast/2FM/. E-mail: (general, Web radio) 2fm@websters.ie; (studio) 2fm@iol.ie; (technical problems) live@websters.ie; (requests and feedback) http://live.websters.ie/broadcast/2FM/feedback.html.

INTERNATIONAL

⊠ (RA44) **Radio Telefís Eireann.**
English and Irish news streamed and via file download for an overseas audience. URL: http://www.wrn.org/stations/rte.html. E-mail: boydw@tv.rte.ie.

Italy

World Time +1 (+2 midyear)

☞ With over 2,000 private FM stations, plus RAI, it's not surprising that Italy is active in Web radio, especially in the north. Some of the offerings are excellent, but so far no stations from Sicily are available.

LOCAL

Cuneo
(RA44) **Radio Stereo 5 *FM 100.6*.** On-demand local and national news and sports, along with a wide variety of features, all presented in Italian from the northeastern part of the country

near today's French border. URL: Cuneo—http://www.cuneo.alpcom.it/ra/realaudio.html. E-mail: radio.stereo5@cuneo.alpcom.it.

Lugano

(RA288) mono **(RA44) Università della Svizzera italana.** On-demand discussions in Italian on a variety of topics. URL: http://www.rtsi.ch/rete2/osserva/osserva.htm. E-mail: rete2@rtsi.ch.

Padova

(RA44) Radiopadova. American, Italian and other pop and rock in an American-style format, as well as news—all presented live in Italian from a station with FM transmitters scattered throughout northwestern Italy. URL: http://intercity.shiny.it/radiopd/rpdlive.html. E-mail (in Italian or English): (general) radiopadova@intercity.shiny.it; (administration) p.mursiz@intercity.shiny.it.

Rome

(RA44) Radio Dimensione Suono Network. Rock music and dedications, presented in Italian. URL: http://www.fnc.net/fnc/rds-live.htm or http://www.fnc.net:80/fnc/rds-live.htm. E-mail: info@flashnet.it.

(RA44) Radio Radio F.M. 104.5. Claims to be the number one talk radio station in Italy, covering a wide range of subjects from football to opera—all live and in Italian, of course. URL: http://

www.radioradio.it. E-mail: posta@radioradio.it. Phone-in line: +39 (6) 880-5241/2.

Sardinia

(RA288) mono **(RA44) Radiolina, la Radio che "fa radio,"** Cagliari. This station, with FM transmitters throughout Sardinia, offers only on-demand audio clips of newly released Italian popular songs ("*Italiana È Bello Della Settimana*"); also, check text page for the occasional sports interview in Italian. As to the possibility of live audio, Radiolina's Marcello Mascia states, "we hope to do this in 1997 if we can obtain a sponsor that offers us money to obtain streamed RealAudio." URL: (songs) http://www.vol.it/RADIOLINA/itbell.htm; (text and audio sports interview) http://www.vol.it/RADIOLINA/index.htm. E-mail: radio@vol.it.

(RA288) mono **(RA44) Radio X FM 96.8**, Cagliari. Boyz II Bambini? You'd hardly expect Hip-Hop Heaven to be in Sardinia, Italy, but here it is: first-rate live and on-demand American black music, mainly hip-hop/trip-hop/rap, along with soul and funk, plus some R&B and jazz. All presented in Italian, adding to the surreal effect. URL: http://www.vol.it/UK/EN/SPETTACOLI/RADIOX/. E-mail (in Italian or English): sergio@vol.it.

Vicenza

(RA288) mono **Radio Vicenza 103.2 La tua citta' in FM.** On-demand morning and evening news headlines in Italian from this station in northwestern Italy.

Kårstein Eidem Løvaas was educated in New Orleans and holds a degree in Political Economics. He's now heard over Norway's Radio Hele Norge P4, which may expand its Web radio operation in 1997.

URL: http://www.radiovicenza.it/html/info.htm. E-mail: webmaster@qestel.it.

NATIONAL AND INTERNATIONAL

IRRS Globe Radio Milano/Shortwave. Live material in Italian, English and other languages, including United Nations/UNESCO Radio (see **United Nations**). URL: http://www.nexus.org/IRN/ or http://home.nexus.org/IRN/. E-mail: info@nexus.org.

RAI RTV Italiana. RAI tends to get an unfairly negative press in Italy, when in reality it is outstanding in certain technical and other respects. Currently, they are working up a tasteful Web site that includes the overseas and many domestic networks RAI operates. Bits of on-demand audio are already available via file download, and in due course high-quality streamed audio is expected to emerge in Italian, English and a host of other languages. Stay tuned! URL: (home page to the various networks) http://www.rai.it/. E-mail: available off the network pages you select.

Norway

World Time +1 (+2 midyear)

NATIONAL

Radio Hele Norge P4. On-demand hourly news in Norwegian from what is otherwise a rock and pop station with a network of some 90 FM transmitters throughout Norway, plus one in Göteborg, Sweden. Regular live transmissions have ceased for the time being, but might resume sometime in 1997. However, there continue to be occasional live broadcasts. URL: (on-demand audio) http://www.p4.no/nyheter/p4lyd/; (occasional live audio) http://www.p4.no/live. E-mail: (English or Norwegian) roy.hovdan@p4.no or p4@p4.no.

LOCAL

Oslo
RaDIO TaNGO FM 99.3. mono Rock and alternative rock presented

live in Norwegian for several hours each day in segments. URL: (audio) http://www.radiotango.no/realtango.html (click on LIVE atop page); (Web Radio schedule, in Oslo Time) http://www.radiotango.no/sverre/info.html. E-mail: radiotango@radiotango.no or sverre@radiotango.no.

Poland

World Time +1 (+2 midyear)

LOCAL

Kraków

RA288 mono **Radio Akademickie Kraków RAK 100.5 FM.** News, sports, financial reports, comedy and music, live in Polish. URL: (audio) http://ituner.com/530AM/; (station) http://galaxy.uci.agh.edu.pl/~rak/. E-mail: (station) rak@uci.agh.edu.pl; (Webmaster) prt@ituner.com.

NATIONAL

RA288 stereo **Polskie Radio Trojka.** The Third Program, in Polish. URL: http://www.radio.com.pl/trojka/internoc/. E-mail: internoc@radio.com.pl.

INTERNATIONAL

⊠ **RA44** **Polish Radio Warsaw Polskie Radio 5.** On-demand news in English and Polish. URL: http://www.wrn.org/stations/poland.html. E-mail: rafalk@radio.com.pl.

Portugal

World Time +1 (+2 midyear); Azores World Time −1 (World Time midyear)

LOCAL/NATIONAL

RA44 **Rádio Comercial**, Lisbon. News, sports activities, Christian programs and live soccer in Portuguese 24 hours a day, along with a wide range of on-demand material. URL: http://www.radiocomercial.pt/audio/audio.html. E-mail: comprot@telepac.pt.

RA44 **TVi** *Televisão Independente.* On-demand cable-TV audio, with Portuguese-language news and weather (Novo Jornal) for continental Portugal, the Azores and Madeira. URL: http://www.tvi-online.com/versao2x/mainframe.html. E-mail: webmaster@cibertribe.pt.

Romania

World Time +2 (+3 midyear)

⊠ **RA44** **Radio Romãnia International.** News in English from Romania's official international broadcaster. URL: http://www.wrn.org/stations/romania.html. E-mail: rador@radio.ror.ro or ri@radio.ror.ro.

Russia

World Time +2 (+3 midyear) Moscow-St. Petersburg; elsewhere, to +13 (+14 midyear)

LOCAL

Moscow

Open Radio *FM 102.5 MHz AM 918 kHz.* This station is considering Web radio, but the Webmaster first wants comments from potential listeners. URL: http://www.openradio.ru/. E-mail: (Webmaster, in English or Russian) webmaster@openradio.ru; (programs) editor@openradio.ru; (listener survey in Russian) http://www.openradio.ru/opros.asp.
.wav .au **Radio Maximum *103.7 FM.*** Western and Russian pop, but only on-demand hit songs are offered—none streamed—in this marginal Web operation. URL: http://www.maximum.ru/mainmenu/html. E-mail: maximum@online.ru.
Shockwave LiveMedia **Radio 101 *101.2 FM.*** Russian and Western rock clips, but so far nothing live. URL: http://www.101.ru/. E-mail: ady@demos.su or http://www.101.ru/mail.htm.
RA44 **Radio Panorama *PC 106.8.*** When operating. URL: http://www.station.ru/. E-mail: radio@station.ru.
RA288 mono **Radio Racurs *792 kHz AM.*** Russian and Western pop, rock and oldies. URL: http://www.music.ru/. E-mail: admin@rinet.ru.
RA44 **Radio Station Silver Rain 100.1 MHz FM *Radiostansiya***

Serebryanyy Dozhid. Russian and Western rock, hip hop and pop. URL: (click last icon on page) http://www.tsr.ru:8082/. E-mail: may@tsr.ru.

St. Petersburg-Petrograd

RA44 **Radio 1 Petrograd *FM 71,66 MHz.*** Russian and Western rock, live and on-demand from this spirited Russian-American operation. URL: (live, 14.4 kb) http://mayday.freelines.ru/rafiles/radio1.ram; (on-demand, eventually also live at 14.4 and 28.8 kb) http://www.freelines.ru/art/music/radio1/r1_e.htm. E-mail: radio1@infopro.spb.su.
.wav .au **Radio Maximum *102.8 FM*, St. Petersburg.** See Moscow, above, where main station is located.

INTERNATIONAL

⊠ *RA44* **Voice of Russia.** On-demand news in English from Russia's official international broadcaster, formerly known as Radio Moscow, streamed and via file download. URL: http://www.wrn.org/stations/vor. E-mail: letters@vor.ru.

Slovak Republic (Slovakia)

World Time +1 (+2 midyear)

Bratislava/Banska Bystrica/Sitno

RA44 **Radio Twist *101.8 FM.*** On-demand news and features in Slovak via RealAudio and file download direct from Slovakia and two North

American sites. URL: (direct RealAudio plus FTP Canadian link) http://www.eunet.sk/twist/twist.html; (RealAudio from United States plus FTP Canadian link) http://www.ituner.com/more_twist.htm. E-mail: sds@slovakia.eu.net or ivan@slovakia.eu.net; (ituner in Canada) ee-radio@ituner.com.

Spain

World Time +1 (+2 midyear)

Barcelona

RA44 Catalunya Informació *Xarxa 4*. News, weather, soccer and sports results, live and on-demand, in the Catalan language from this regional public station. URL: (live) http://www.catradio.es/cr/cr-direc.html; (on-demand) http://www.catradio.es/cr/cr-carta.html. E-mail: being installed.

RA44 Catalunya Ràdio *Xarxa 1*. Dramas and other features, live and on-demand, in the Catalan language from this regional public station. Also see **3ZZZ, Melbourne, Australia**. URL: (live) http://www.catradio.es/cr/cr-direc.html; (on-demand) http://www.catradio.es/cr/cr-carta.html. E-mail: being installed.

RA44 COM Ràdio *Els matins amb Josep Cuní*. On-demand news and features in the Catalan language, aired on FM and mediumwave AM throughout Cataluña. URL: http://www.partal.com/cuni/. E-mail: acl@bcn.servicom.es.

Madrid

RA44 Radio Intereconomía 95.1 FM. On-demand economic news and market report in Spanish. URL: http://negocios.com/ie/real2.htm. E-mail: gnegocios@bitmailer.com.

Santiago de Compostela

RA44 Radio Galega. A wide variety of feature programs and live football in Galician. URL: http://www.crtvg.es/. E-mail: crtvg@crtvg.es.

Sweden

World Time +1 (+2 midyear)

LOCAL

Stockholm

RA288 mono **Bandit *105.5 Rock*.** Today's rock, live, presented in Swedish in predictable formula fashion. URL: http://www.bandit.se/. E-mail: nv95wahe@linnea.asogy.stockholm.se.

StreamWorks 2.0 **Power 106.3.** Live hip hop, funk and soul, presented in Swedish. Some of the cuts contain language that keeps them off the air on most American stations. URL: http://www.power106.telegate.se/live.html.

RA44 Radio Rix. When it is actually functioning, the day's news headlines are available on-demand in Swedish via streamed RealAudio and file download. URL: http://

R. Argovia

Christian Stärkle heads Swiss Radio Argovia, which since 1990 has transmitted rock and news in Schweizerdeutsch throught Aargau-Baden.

www.everyday.se/radiorix/. E-mail: webmaster@everyday.com.

StreamWorks 2.0 **Vinyl 107.1.** One of the best oldies station on the Web! Rock and some pop, mostly American and British and nominally from the Sixties and Seventies, but some of their best stuff is actually from the Fifties. Pleasantly presented in Swedish with relatively few commercial or other obnoxious intrusions, making this a first-rate choice for oldies fans weary of high-chatter American stations . . . *when* StreamWorks is in an "un-hiccupy" mood. URL: http://www.vinyl107.telegate.se/live.html. E-mail (requests and comments): http://www.vinyl107.telegate.se/vad.html.

NATIONAL

RA288 mono **Sveriges Radio.** On-demand news in Swedish from the P1 and P3

networks. URL: http://www.sr.se/ekot/nyheter/. E-mail: (programs) prof@sr.se; (Webmaster) webmaster@eko.sr.se.

INTERNATIONAL

RA44 **Radio Sweden.** On-demand news and features in English, Swedish, German and Russian in RealAudio, with English also via file download. URL: (all languages and programs) http://www.sr.se/rs/realaudi.htm; (English news and MediaScan program only) http://www.wrn.org/stations/rs.html; (Swedish news only) http://www.sr.se/rs/svenska/nyheter.htm; (a day's worth of Swedish "Dagens Eko" 3-30 minute radio newsreels only) http://www.sr.se/rs/ekot/nyheter/. E-mail: info@rs.sr.se.

Switzerland

World Time +1 (+2 midyear)

LOCAL

Brugg (Aargau-Baden)

RA288 mono **Radio Argovia 90,3+94,9.** Today's rock, plus lots of newscasts, live in Schweizerdeutsch. URL: (click on station logo) http://www.winet.ch/argovia/. E-mail: (station) argovia@winet.ch; (Webmaster) admin@winet.ch.

Rapperswil (Zürich)

RA288 mono **Radio Zürisee.** Pop, light rock and oldies, along with regional and other news and features, including sports. It's all presented live in Schweizerdeutsch on RealAudio, plus jingles via file download, from this station with FM transmitters and cable-radio service throughout the Zürich region. URL: http://www.world.ch/radio/online/. E-mail: radio@world.ch.

United Kingdom

World Time exactly (+1 midyear)

NATIONAL

RA288 mono **RA44** **IRN Independent Radio News/SMS Satellite Media Services**, London. The latest IRN news (14.4), plus bloopers and DJ clips (28.8)—all on-demand. URL: http://www.sms.co.uk/real.html. E-mail: info@sms.co.uk.

RA288 stereo **RA288** mono **Virgin Radio**, London. If you have to ask what this station's about, you don't want to know. The best Web radio offering from the U.K., with REM and other special concert transmissions thrown in every now and then (look at the bottom of the Web page). URL: http://www.virginradio.co.uk/radio.html. E-mail: http://www.virginradio.co.uk/reception_visitors.html.

NATIONAL/INTERNATIONAL

☒ **RA44** **BBC**, London. The Flat Earth Society for Third-Wave Communications *1997 Award for Bandwidth Conservation* goes to . . . Auntie Beeb, the Lady Laryngitis of London, with her solitary offering of three on-demand clips of the defunct "Andrew Neil Show." If listeners aren't naughty, for 1998 they may also get to hear several reruns of "Listen with Mother" from 1950. URL: (final Neil Show) http://www.bbc.co.uk/andrewneil/; (two February, 1996, Neil Shows) http://www.bbc.co.uk/andrewneil/archive/index.html. E-mail: correspondence@bbc.co.uk.

RA288 mono **Financial Times Television and Radio.** A wide variety of world and financial news and features are aired. Given the quality of their output, this is a most attractive spot for business, economic and world

BRITISH BROADCASTING CORPORATION WORLD SERVICE

The BBC World Service is the ultimate broadcaster in the English language. For now, it has little on Web radio, but expansion is possible. However, it is heard worldwide, night and day, over world band radio.

Listen... as history unfolds.

Unparalleled news and perspectives, plus every sort of music and diversion: That's world band radio, from as many as 165 countries.

PASSPORT TO WORLD BAND RADIO is jammed with just what you need to eavesdrop on this world: Best and worst radios (**PASSPORT REPORTS**). Station and Internet addresses and giveaways (Addresses PLUS).

Schedules, too – the way you want them. What shows are on, hour by hour (What's on Tonight)... country by country (Worldwide Broadcasts in English and Voices from Home)... frequency by frequency (the renowned Blue Pages).

With **PASSPORT**, you'll have the world at your fingertips.

Fully revised and greatly expanded for 1997.

Over 600,000 copies sold worldwide.

Exceptionally handy for day-to-day use.

PASSPORT TO WORLD BAND RADIO
The must-have guide to your must-hear world.

ISBN 0-914941-39-9

Available from dealers and bookstores throughout the United States, Canada and the United Kingdom, or write:

IBS, Box 300, Penn's Park, PA 18943 USA
http://www.passport.com/
e-mail: mwk@passport.com

news. Except for the end-of-day roundup, all programs are in 28.8 only; however, they expect to drop 14.4 altogether before long. URL: ("RA" logo contiguous to where to click for RealAudio) http://www.ft-television.com/. E-mail: (general) comments@ ftvision.com; (Webmaster) tom@ftvision.com.

INTERNATIONAL

RA44 MTA *Muslim Television Ahmadiyya*. Live and on-demand Muslim sermons, talks, education and music, mostly in Urdu but occasionally in English, from this satellite-fed network for Pakistanis worldwide. URL: http://www.alislam.org/audio/. E-mail: info@islam.alislam.org.

RA44 World Radio Network Gateway to International Public Radio, London. Hyperlink to various government-sponsored international radio broadcasters, either streamed or via file download. URL: http://www.wrn.org/audio.html or http://town.hall.org/Archives/radio/Mirrors/WRN/index.html. E-mail: online@wrn.org.

Vatican City State

World Time +1 (+2 midyear)

RA44 Vatican Radio. On-demand news and features in English, plus news in French and German, streamed and via file download. Also, various streamed audio clips in English. URL: (news and features) http://wrn.org/stations/vatican.html; (audio clips)

Digital Stock

Vatican Radio goes way back, being inaugurated in 1931 by Guglielmo Marconi and Pope Pius XI. It has made a major commitment to Web radio.

http://www.wrn.org/vatican-radio/. E-mail: mc6778@mclink.it.

Yugoslavia

World Time +1 (+2 midyear)

Belgrade

RA44 Radio B92. On-demand news in English and Serbian, but plans to go live soon. URL: http://www.xs4all.nl/~opennet/audio.html. E-mail: matic@b92.opennet.org.

Prepared by the staff of PASSPORT TO WEB RADIO.

Web Radio from Africa, Asia and the Pacific

Most of the world's population lives "East of Suez," as the British once put it—or to the south. Yet, until Web radio came into being, it was not always easy to keep in direct touch with the goings-on in this part of the world.

You can now tune into these lands and peoples instantaneously and at little cost. From the home of the wallabies to the heart of South Africa, from the historic Levant to the "Tigers" of Asia, their world is within your reach.

World Time +11 (+10 midyear) Victoria (VIC), New South Wales (NSW), Australian Capital Territory (ACT) and Tasmania (TAS); +10:30 (+9:30 midyear) South Australia (SA); +10 Queensland (QLD); +9:30 Northern Territory (NT); +8 Western Australia (WA)

LOCAL

Adelaide

RA288 mono **Radio 5UV 531 AM Adelaide University.** Jazz, classical, country, folk, oldies and other music, along with a wide range of feature programs. URL: http://www.adelaide.edu.au/5UV/broadcast.html. E-mail: wbickley@radio5uv.adelaide.edu.au.

Korean countryside in autumn.   Korean Information Center

Radio Television Hong Kong isn't heard live, but instead has a wide range of on-demand programs. These include news in English and Cantonese, as well as Chinese pop music.

Melbourne

(RA288) mono KISS 90 FM (when active). "Serious dance" music is the way they describe their mix of rave, hip-hop and other offerings. In principle, they are live, but don't be surprised if all you can unearth are on-demand clips. URL: (home) http://www.kiss.sprint.com.au/main.html or http://www.kiss.sprint.com.au/KISS90.html; (Net Update, on-demand) http://www.peg.apc.org/toysatellite/netupdate/. E-mail: (general) kissstaff@kiss.sprint.com.au; (Net Update) toysatellite@peg.apc.org; (Webmaster) kissweb.sprint.com.au.

(RA288) mono (RA44) Fox-FM Today's 101.9 FM. On-demand top-40 rock music, net@nite show, news and various DJ clips. More serious on-demand news is about to be added, but as of when we go to press the net@nite show is the only offering of more than passing interest. URL: (general) http://www.fox.com.au/ or http://www.village.com.au/airwaves/austereo/fox/fox.htm; (net@nite) http://www.village.com.au/airwaves/austereo/net_nite/net_nite.htm. E-mail: fox_fm@village.com.au.

(RA44) 3ZZZ-FM Radiodifusió Catalana (if activated). "Hope to have RealAudio facility soon," according to Josep Viñas, Webmaster of this unusual site. News from Catalonia, Catalan music and other items in the Catalan language of Spain. (Yes, you read that correctly—there is a substantial expatratiate Spanish community in Melbourne.) URL: http://www.sustance.com/catalan/index.html. E-mail: jovinas@melbpc.org.au.

Sydney

RA288 mono **KICK-AM 1269.** Country, blues and Cajun music, as well as AFL football coverage and surfing/fishing reports. As of when we go to press, KICK's RealAudio server has not been functioning, but the station says it will be up and running properly before long. URL: http://www.kick-am.com.au/javaindex.html. E-mail: (general) contact@kick-am.com.au or trevor@kick-am.com.au; (Webmaster) natasha@kick-am.com.au.

NATIONAL

RA288 mono **Austereo Network/Channel Seven Network** *Global Environmental News.* On-demand weekly half-hour of thought-provoking environmental news and interviews from Planet ARK, in cooperation with the Austereo (radio) Network and the Seven (TV) Network, which have FM, VHF and UHF outlets throughout much of Australia. Nicely presented, and refreshing free from political dogmatism—well worth hearing. URL: http://www.planet.ark.com.au/netradio.html. E-mail: admin@planet.ark.com.au.

INTERNATIONAL

RA44 **Radio Australia ABC.** On-demand news and features—notably about Australia, Asia and the Pa-

cific—from Australia's official international broadcaster. URL (RealAudio, streamed, and file download): http://www.wrn.org/stations/abc.html or http://www.abc.net.au/ra/elp/elpwrn.htm. E-mail: (Webmaster) naughton.russell@a2.abc.net.au; (English Service) raelp@radioaus.abc.net.au; (other) ratx@radioaus.abc.net.au, raust3@ozemail.com.au or http://www.abc.net.au/ra/res/contact.htm.

China (Hong Kong)

World Time +8

RA44 **Hong Kong Commercial Radio.** Modern Chinese music and news in Cantonese. URL: http://www.asiaonline.net/comradio/lt881.htm. E-mail: comradio@asiaonline.net.

RA44 **Metro Plus 1044 AM.** Music and news in English and Mandarin. URL: http://www.metroradio.com.hk or http://www.asiaonline.net/metro. E-mail: (Webmaster) bob@metroradio.com.hk.

RA44 **104 FM Select.** Music and news in English and Cantonese. URL: http://www.metroradio.com.hk or http://www.asiaonline.net/metro. E-mail: (station) fmselect@metroradio.com.hk; (Webmaster) bob@metroradio.com.hk.

RA44 **RA288** mono **Radio Television Hong Kong.** Authoritative news in English, as well as a wide variety of music and information programs in Cantonese.

Metro Broadcast

Steve James and Harry Wong keep Hong Kong's 104 FM Select a lively place to hang out—whether you speak English or Cantonese.

All programs, on-demand, are currently in RealAudio 14.4 v2.0; however, the Chinese Pop Chart is also available in 28.8 v2.0 and v3.0. URL (RealAudio and file downloads): (all languages and services, menu selectable) http://www.cuhk.hk/cgi-custom/rthk/newsindex.pl, http://www.iponline.com/rthk/index.html or http://www.cuhk.hk/rthk/; (English news on Monday-Friday only) http://www.wrn.org/stations/rthk.html. E-mail: jmfcheng@super.net or http://www.cuhk.hk/rthk/feedback.html.

China (Taiwan)

World Time +8

RA14.4 **BCC Broadcasting Corporation of China.** News in Mandarin, at times when it is being put out over Web radio. Also, ID clips in various languages from each of the stations within the BCC organization. URL: (for news, click on RealAudio icon in mid-page; for IDs, click on desired station's icon along right side of page) http://www.bcc.com.tw/. E-mail: (click on station you wish to contact) http://www.bcc.com.tw/message/message.htm.

StreamWorks 2.0 **International Community Radio Taipei FM 100.7.** Modern Western and Chinese music presented in English, with some Mandarin. URL: http://www.icrt.com.tw/FFen_live.htm or http://www.icrt.com.tw/ or http://www.icrt.com.tw/_framestart.htm. E-mail: comments@icrt.tw.

RA28.8 mono .au **Philharmonic Radio Taipei PRT FM99.7.** A most pleasant station for Western classical music and jazz, with announcements in Mandarin Chinese, although the audio quality will benefit greatly when the station eventually upgrades to RealAudio v3.0. (Currently, it's v2.0, which doesn't hack it with *fortissimo* passages unless your eardrums are made of rawhide.) Nominally live, but don't be surprised to find it's actually time-delayed, possibly so Web listeners don't start listening in the middle of a long concert. Also offered are .au downloaded files of voice clips. URL: ("live," click on RealAudio icon) http://www.prtmusic.com.tw/News; (.au voice clips) http://www.prtmusic.com.tw/Voice/people.html. E-mail: prtweb@prtmusic.com.tw.

RA44 Voice of Taipei 107.7 MHz. On-demand music, news, sports talk, traffic and comedy in Mandarin Chinese. However, you first need to obtain an alias and password to listen for something like two days, after which you have to pay $3 to $4 per month. URL: http://ww3.sinanet.com/vot/html/index.html. E-mail: info@sinanet.com.

YTN is one of the Republic of Korea's main sources for television news. It's heard worldwide on the Web with live audio.

India

World Time +5:30

RA44 All India Internet Radio. Twenty-odd minutes of on-demand English-language news about India with stock market report, primarily for Indians abroad, but also for the rest of the world's population, from this Internet-only commercial station that shouldn't be confused with India's official All India Radio (below) that also plans to be on Web radio before long. Also, a variety of on-demand features, including lovely Indian music, in English and Hindi—mostly streamed, but partly via file download. URL: (with frames) http://www.aiir.com/aiir/aiir2.htm?; (without frames) http://www.aiir.com/cgi-bin/aiirfile.bat?aiir2.html; (English news only) http://www.aiir.com/aiir/nw-ne.html. E-mail: cyberjockey@aiir.com, dharam@aiir.com, rajeev@aiir.com or http://www.aiir.com/cgi-bin/aiirfile.bat?yu-about.html.

RA44 All India Radio. This huge government operation, the only broadcaster currently allowed to operate in India, will be active very shortly on Web radio. Likely to be aired are news and features in, at a minimum, English and Hindi, targeted both to foreigners and Indians abroad. URL: (home page) http://air.kode.net/. E-mail: rdair@giasdl01.vsnl.net.in or http://air.kode.net/feedback.html.

Iran

World Time +3:30

mono **Voice of the Islamic Republic of Iran.** The latest VOIRI Per-

到底好了吗。。。

就快了

SAFRA

If you want to enjoy today's Chinese pop music, click on Dongli 88.3 FM from Singapore. Be sure to download StreamWords software beforehand.

sian-language news on-demand from Tehran. Also, archived Persian traditional music that's well worth hearing. URL: http://netiran.com/ PersianRadio.html. E-mail: (general) irib@dci.iran.com; (Research Centre) iribrec@dci.iran.com.

Israel

World Time +2 (+3 midyear)

Internet Wave RA44 **Kol Israel (IBA).** News in English, as well as news and news-related features in Hebrew from

Kol Israel's Reshet Bet domestic service and audio from a cable-TV channel. All programs are on-demand, with Internet Wave requiring no file download. Alas, for whatever perverse reason RealAudio is offered by file download only, with no streaming, but ignore Artificia's instructions which imply that PC users can't use RealAudio—it works just fine, even though the English news and some programs are offered *only* in Internet Wave. (Have fun getting this to work on Internet Explorer 3.0!) URL: http://www.artificia.com/html/news.cgi or http://virtual.co.il/city_services/news/kol.htm. E-mail: ask@israel-info.gov.il, art@artificia.com or http://www.artificia.com/html/feedback.htm.

Japan

World Time +9

☞ You might think Japan, with its computer industry and expatriates worldwide, would be a hotbed of Web radio activity, but it isn't. Nary a station airs fulltime streamed audio, and even on-demand offerings are sparse.

LOCAL

Hayama

(RA288) mono **(stereo with ISDN) Shonan Beach FM 78.9.** On-demand jazz, presented in Japanese. URL: http://www.beachfm.co.jp/jazz/jazzweb.html. E-mail: http://www.beachfm.co.jp/letter/index.html.

Hiroshima

(RA44) **VDOLive JOER *RCC Radio 1350.*** All that this AM station's Web site airs live are Tokyo Carp baseball games, presented in Japanese. However, there's also on-demand audio in English and Japanese concerning the 1945 atomic bombings of Hiroshima and Nagasaki. URL: http://www.rcc-hiroshima.co.jp/. E-mail: rcc@rcc-hiroshima.co.jp.

Kyoto

(RA288) mono **Shockwave Station "i".** Various offerings, but little audio, exclusively in Japanese via this Web-only station that's definitely no grabber. URL: http://www.age.or.jp/station-i/. E-mail: station@age.or.jp or http://www.age.or.jp/station-i/welcome/form.html.

Osaka

(RA288) mono **StreamWorks** 1.0 **JOFV *Funky 802 FM.*** Top 100 pop and rock hits from today and the recent past, presented live in Japanese for selected time slots during most days of the week. Also, audio clips of deejay voices in RealAudio and via file download. URL: (graphics) http://www.fm802.co.jp/graphicindex.html or (sans graphics) http://www.fm802.co.jp/textindex.html. E-mail: http://www.fm802.co.jp/dear802/index.html.

The staff of Manila's DWCT-FM "City Lite 88.3" offers relaxing music and business headlines, all live and in English.

Tokyo

RA44 **JOAU Tokyo FM 80.0 MHz.** The latest in the world's music and information, in Japanese and on-demand. URL: http://www.ipgn.com/audio/index-e.html. E-mail: i-radio@impress.co.jp.

RA288 mono **JOAV J-WAVE 81.3 FM.** Japanese pop music on-demand clips only, but station wants feedback so it can decide whether to expand its Web radio offerings. URL: http://www.infojapan.com/JWAVE/. E-mail: (English) http://www.infojapan.com/JWAVE/dear_j-wave-e.html; (Japanese) http://www.infojapan.com/JWAVE/dear_j-wave.html.

RA44 **JOLF 1242 AM Nippon Broadcasting System.** Only J.League soccer in Japanese. URL: http://www.ipgn.com/JOLF/index-e.html. E-mail: (station) http://www.fujisankei-g.co.jp/jolf/mailtop.htm; (J. League) j-league@www.dentsu.co.jp.

<hr>

Korea (Republic)

World Time +9

LOCAL/NATIONAL

RA44 **MBC AM Radio 900**, Seoul. Korean pop and rock music and news live from the Munhwa Broadcasting Corporation, Korea's largest commercial radio network, with transmitters throughout the country. URL: http://

www.mbc.com.kr/real.htm. E-mail:
mbcsysop@mbc.co.kr.

StreamWorks 2.0 **YTN-TV Cable Channel 24**,
Seoul. Yonhap News Agency's live TV
audio in Korean, at hours when available. URL: http://www.ytn.co.kr/
ytn10.htm. E-mail: http://
www.ytn.co.kr/ytn12.htm (specify
"YTN-10 Webmaster" in your subject
or name line).

INTERNATIONAL

RA44 **Radio Korea International
(KBS).** On-demand news in English
and Korean from this country's official
international broadcaster. Via
streamed RealAudio and file download. URL: (English) http://
kbsnt.kbs.co.kr/pr/rkinews.htm;
(Korean) http://kbsnt.kbs.co.kr/pr/
test1.htm; (English and Korean) http://
www.wrn.org/stations/kbs.html.
E-mail: pr@kbsnt.co.kr,
info@kbsnt.kbs.co.kr or
webmaster@kbsnt.kbs.co.kr.

Malaysia

World Time +8

☞ The little nation with a big voice,
multi-ethnic Malaysia makes a fine
showing on the Web, including over
RTM's Radio Muzik and other networks that air Asian songs you're unlikely to hear anywhere else. The only
hitch: Bandwidth limitations from the

RTM site sometimes cause gaps of
silence while the audio tries to catch
up by buffering.

LOCAL/NATIONAL

RA288 mono **RA44** **RTM Radio Televisyen
Malaysia**, Kuala Lumpur. Web radio
just doesn't get much better than this
government-owned operation, with no
less than *six* live RTM network feeds
usually available round-the-clock
from RTM's one Web site: **Radio 4**
(**RA44** 100.1 FM in KL) nationwide in
with pop and rock music and news in
English; the pleasant **Radio Muzik**
(**RA288** 95.3 FM in KL) with nonstop,
mostly Asian, pop and rock music
introduced in Bahasa Malaysia;
Radio KL (**RA44** 97.2 FM) operating
most of the day for Kuala Lumpur,
with Western and other rock and pop
and news; **Radio 1** (**RA44** 98.3 FM in
KL) nationwide with Malaysian music,
news and Islamic programming in
Bahasa Malaysia; **Radio 5** (**RA44**
106.7 FM in KL) nationwide with
Chinese music, news and chat in
Mandarin (Standard Chinese); and
Radio 6 (**RA44** 96.3 FM in KL) nationwide with Indian music, news and
talk in Tamil. Watch for the URL to
change, hopefully with more bandwidth, although the current URL
should forward for some time to come.
URL: http://www.asiaconnect.com.my/
rtm-net/live/. E-mail: http://
www.asiaconnect.com.my/rtm-net/
guest/.

Carole Hisasue, raised and educated in California, divides her time between Tokyo's "J-WAVE 81.3 FM" and producing television programs. The station hopes for feedback from listeners to decide whether to expand its Web radio offerings.

RA44 **Time Highway Radio**, Kuala Lumpur. Live and on-demand pop, rock and alternative rock from Asia, America and beyond in English, plus news, from this mainly private, partly government-owned station with FM transmitters throughout much of the country. URL: (live) http://thr.time.com.my/; (on-demand) http://thr.time.com.my/program.html; (deejay audio clips) http://thr.time.com.my/djs.html. E-mail: (general) webmaster@thr.time.com.my; (deejays) albertng@hotmail.com.

World Time +8

☞ Filipino expats abound in North America, the Middle East and beyond, forming a potentially huge audience for Filipino Web radio stations. The only one currently on the air started in October, 1996, but offers little other than everyday "lite" music. Look for this roster to expand to include stations with more localized news and other original programming.

LOCAL

Manila

RA288 mono **DWCT-FM** *City Lite 88.3.* Western-style pop music and soft jazz, presented live in English with some ads in Tagalog, from a station that sounds like it could come from Anywhere. Business news, traffic reports and not much else except lots and lots of ads. On-demand audio clips are to be added in the near future. URL: http://www.wtouch.com.ph/~citylite/main.htm. E-mail: (station) ctguests@wtouch.com.ph; (Webmaster)ctwebber@wtouch.com.ph.

Singapore

World Time +8

☞ Although Singapore's present Web radio offerings are limited, there are indications that this may improve before long.

index.htm. E-mail: michaelk@pacific.net.sg.

NATIONAL

StreamWorks 2.0 **Dongli 88.3 FM.** Pop music in Mandarin Chinese from the SAFRA (Singaporan Armed Forces Reservist Association) Radio Group. URL: (click on red panel with Chinese characters) http://www.fm883.com.sg/live.html. E-mail: (general) fm883@pacific.net.sg; (popularity vote) http://www.fm883.com.sg/vote.html.

RA288 mono **RA44 RCS City Sounds 93.3.** Audio clips of a small number of Chinese pop hits. URL: http://www.mediacity.com.sg/radio/rcs/933/1997/clips.htm. E-mail: fm933@pacific.net.sg.

RA288 mono **RCS Perfect Ten 98.7.** Audio clips and on-demand interviews in English from this hit music station. URL: http://www.mediacity.com.sg/radioct/rcs/p10/1997/audio.htm. E-mail: p10@pacific.net.sg.

RA288 mono **RCS Radio Corporation of Singapore.** Each week, this network airs a substantial on-demand audio offering in English, Chinese, Malay or Tamil from one of its ten stations. URL: (click Now Playing) http://www.mediacity.com.sg/radioct/rcs/

Channel Africa is an outstanding source of information about African current affairs. It plans to further expand its Web radio offerings for 1997.

INTERNATIONAL

.wav RCS Radio Singapore International. News and features are aired worldwide by this, Singapore's official international broadcaster. However, for the present only a couple of audio clips are available on the Web, all via file download. URL: (English) http://www.rsi.com.sg/english/editor/; (Chinese and Malay) http://www.rsi.com.sg/. E-mail: radiosi@singnet.com.sg.

South Africa

World Time +2

LOCAL

Johannesburg

RA288 stereo **RA44 Impact Radio 103 FM Stereo.** Christian popular music, interviews and talks presented in English. RealAudio v3.0 stereo should sound great (sometimes the station is RA 3.0 28.8 stereo, other times RA 2.0 14.4 mono), but not if it's fed

JOFV

Tortoise Matsumoto shells out the latest hits from Osaka's "Funky 802 FM"—one of the few Web radio stations from Japan with regular live programming.

an audio cassette or fly to Jo'burg to tune in this public radio station. URL: http://www.safari.co.za/. E-mail: ok@safari.co.za.

INTERNATIONAL

⊠ **(RA44)** **Channel Africa.** On-demand news and "Dateline Africa" in English, streamed and via file download. This station is the best source on Web radio on African affairs, which otherwise are sadly ignored by Western mdeia except during famines and civil disturbances. Although strained finances emperil Channel Africa's very existence, it continues to be funded for the moment. URL: http://www.wrn.org/stations/africa.html. E-mail: vorstern@sabc.co.za.

Thailand

World Time +7

LOCAL

Bangkok

(RA288) mono **MCOT FM 97.5 MHz Manager Radio.** A wide variety of on-demand news, cultural affairs and other verbal features in Thai. URL: http://www2.asiaaccess.net.th/mradio/. E-mail: http://www2.asiaaccess.net.th/mradio/html/suggest.html.

a poor signal, and this station can sound like a badly worn Edison cylinder. URL: http://www.qdata.net/~duncanm/impact/. E-mail: (station) info@qdata.co.za; (Webmaster) duncanm@qdata.co.za.

(RA288) mono **.wav Radio Safari 94.4 FM**, Craighall. Numerous brief (under one minute!) streamed RealAudio and downloaded .wav audio clips on various subjects related to Afro-centric wildlife conservation. If you want to hear more, you'll have to cough up for

From Singapore's tidy urban canyons come live and on-demand programs in English, Mandarin and other languages. The Radio Corporation of Singapore alone has three sites, plus Dongli 88.3 FM is available from the Singaporean Armed Forces. Overleaf: Bustling Seoul, Korea is the home to three Web radio stations with music in Korean and English.   Digital Stock

Ban Hat Yai

RA288 mono **TrueSpeech .wav Fantasy Wave 104.0 FM *Magic Radio.*** Seven groupings of on-demand Thai music and Fifties American oldies, with ads removed. Fantasy Wave, a Thai-Malaysia border station, is operated by one Mr. Koong, the owner of a local nightclub establishment. Magic Radio, operated by hotel owner Mr. Boonchoo, is the name of a show over Fantasy Wave during prime time. The combined programs, in turn, are edited for Web radio by two British gentlemen. No newscasts, but the station hopes to go live on the Web soon. URL: http://www.escati.com/magic_radio.htm. E-mail: (general) message@escati.com; (personal messages) personals@escati.com.

Prepared by the staff of PASSPORT TO WEB RADIO.